Mutual Funds Made Easy!

Gerald W. Perritt

Dearborn
Financial Publishing, Inc.

While a great deal of care has been taken to provide accurate and current information, the ideas, suggestions, general principles and conclusions presented in this text are subject to local, state and federal laws and regulations, court cases and any revisions of same. The reader is thus urged to consult legal counsel regarding any points of law—this publication should not be used as a substitute for competent legal advice.

Senior Associate Editor: Karen A. Christensen
Managing Editor: Jack Kiburz
Editorial Assistant: Stephanie C. Schmidt
Cover Design: S. Laird Jenkins Corporation
Interior Design: Lucy Jenkins

Published by Dearborn Financial Publishing, Inc.

Printed in the United States of America

95 96 97 10 9 8 7 6 5 4 3 2 1

Library of Congress Cataloging-in-Publication Data

Perritt, Gerald W.
Mutual funds made easy! / by Gerald W. Perritt.
p. cm.
Includes index.
ISBN 0-7931-1335-0
1. Mutual funds. I. Title.
HG4530.P434 1995
332.63'27—dc20 95-12130
CIP

Contents

Acknowledgments

In writing this book, I have relied on nearly 25 years of experience gained in studying, teaching and advising individuals about mutual fund investing. Over the years, I have benefitted from the wisdom and willingness of mutual fund advisers, administrators and sponsors who taught me a lot about the nature of the mutual fund business. To these people, of which there are too many to thank individually, I owe a huge debt. In addition, I wish to thank the Investment Company Institute for sharing a wealth of statistics about the mutual fund industry. Much of the material gathered for this book has evolved over the years from my newsletter, *The Mutual Fund Letter.* I wish to thank my editorial staff, especially Michael Corbett and David Kuensey, for its assistance in gathering materials for this effort. Finally, I wish to thank Dianne Chaykin Click, president of The Marketing Arm, for her encouragement and for the contacts that she helped me make among the members of the mutual fund community. Without a doubt, this effort would have never come to fruition without the unselfish efforts of these people.

Gerald W. Perritt
Chicago, Illinois

Preface

Investing in a portfolio of well-managed mutual funds is the key to gaining control of your financial destiny. If you apply the same investment techniques that large pension funds use, you too can take advantage of the opportunities to double or even triple the returns being paid on bank savings accounts and at the same time limit your investment risk. Even if you have only a modest nest egg, you can diversify across a wide spectrum of assets, and you can hire some of the best portfolio managers in the world to assist you in expanding your wealth. However, to obtain the best returns, you have to know where to look. You also need to know how to separate the mutual funds with the best performance potential from the more than 6,000 funds now on the market. In addition, you have to recognize the risks of investing in certain funds and be able to control your exposure to risk.

Mutual Funds Made Easy! will guide you safely and quickly through this maze of mutual fund investing. Drawn from more than 25 years of experience, this book is intended to make mutual fund investing easy for both the novice and the seasoned investor. The first few chapters explain how mutual funds work and how to make them work for you. I then show you step-by-step how to select the funds that will best meet your investment needs and objectives. I also outline the portfolio management strategies practiced by the world's most sophisticated and successful long-term investors. Finally, getting started couldn't be easier. You will find brief descriptions of 100 popular mutual funds along with their toll-free telephone numbers.

Why are mutual funds so popular? During the past 15 years, investors have channeled more of their savings toward mutual funds than anywhere else. In fact, during 1994 total mutual fund assets leaped beyond $2 trillion. That's more money than individuals have on deposit in the nation's commercial banks! Today, more than 30 million households have included one or more mutual funds among their investments. And for many good reasons. No matter if you are setting aside a few dollars each month for your children's college education, contributing to an individual retirement account (IRA) or looking for a better place for your savings, mutual funds are right for you.

The benefits of investing the mutual fund way far outstrip the drawbacks. Mutual funds reduce investment risk because they are diversified. Investing in mutual funds means that you don't need to research dozens or even hundreds of individual stocks; instead, experienced professional managers guide the mutual fund portfolios for you. And mutual funds allow even investors with modest means to select from a wide variety of options that were never before available to them.

However, to reap these benefits and avoid the pitfalls, you must understand what mutual funds can and cannot do. Often, uninformed investors are shocked by their funds' performance. Some investors not only do not earn the returns that they should, they also experience devastating losses as well. *Mutual Funds Made Easy!* will help you identify and reduce the costs of investing, recognize the investment style adopted by particular funds and become aware of the risks that some funds pose.

To become a successful investor, learn all that you can about the investment process and apply tried-and-true investment strategies. The rules of investment success are few but crucial to setting up and managing your successful investing program: Investigate before you invest, diversify your portfolio, reduce the costs of investing, assume only as much risk as you can tolerate and invest for the long term. This book will help you build a portfolio of mutual funds by giving you "smart strategies" for following these guidelines. In short, no matter how experienced you are, this book provides an easy-to-follow road map that will lead you well down the road toward achieving your financial goals.

Mutual Funds in Perspective

We can trace the origins of the modern-day mutual fund back to 19th-century Europe. Although they gained considerable popularity in England a century and a half ago, mutual funds did not reach America's shores until 1924, when Massachusetts Investors Trust, the first open-end mutual fund, was organized. Today, the mutual fund industry has virtually exploded—you can now choose from *more than 6,000 mutual funds,* pursuing nearly every imaginable investment objective.

The Lean Years—A Slow Start

Several major events hampered initial growth in the mutual fund industry: first the stock market crash of 1929, the Great Depression that followed and then the outbreak of World War II. By the late 1940s, fewer than 100 mutual funds existed, with combined assets totaling less than $2 billion.

The "Gold" Rush

Although many mutual fund investors tend to take the widespread availability of funds of all kinds for granted, the industry is still in its infancy. During the first half-century of their existence, mutual funds invested in primarily common stocks and corporate bonds. The first money market mutual fund, The Reserve Fund, was organized in November 1971. Tax-exempt money funds made their initial appearance in 1979. Municipal bond funds debuted in 1977, after the passage of legislation that permitted such funds to pass through their tax-exempt income to shareholders. Long-term U.S. government bond funds came on the scene the same year. International bond funds did not arrive until 1986. The industry's newest addition, ARM funds—bond funds that invest in adjustable-rate mortgages—appeared on the scene in 1990. Figure 1.1 illustrates the growth of mutual funds during the past three decades. At the end of 1970, 10.7 million shareholder accounts held 361 stock, bond and income funds, with combined total assets of $47.6 billion.

S MART STRATEGIES *The rules of investment success are few: Investigate before you invest, diversify your portfolio, reduce the costs of investing, assume only as much risk as you can tolerate and invest for the longer term.*

During the next 23 years, the popularity of mutual funds with all types of investors skyrocketed. Ownership of mutual funds soared from 6 percent of U.S. households in 1980 to 27 percent in 1993 (see Figure 1.2). At year-end 1993, investors could choose from 4,558 stock, bond and money market mutual funds. That number would grow beyond 5,000 the following year—more than twice the number of stocks listed for trading on the New York Stock Exchange!

Total industry assets also expanded dramatically during the last decade and a half, growing from $293 billion in 1983, passing the

FIGURE 1.1 □ Number of Mutual Funds

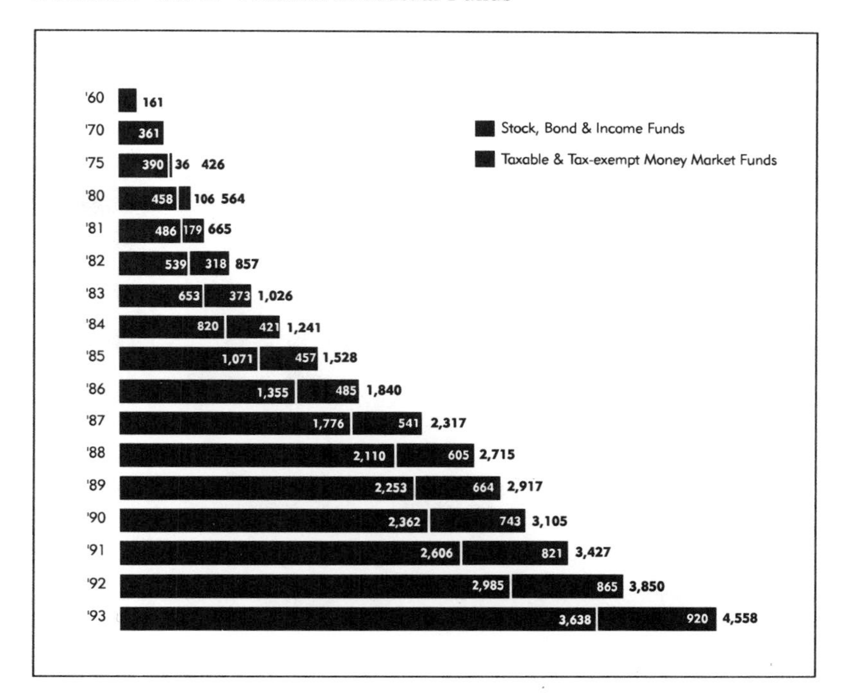

Source: *1994 Mutual Fund Fact Book,* Investment Company Institute, Washington, D.C. Reprinted with permission.

$1 trillion mark in 1990 and surpassing $2 trillion in 1993. In 1994, total mutual fund assets topped the total dollar value of deposits in the nation's commercial banks for the first time ever.

Figure 1.3 contains year-by-year mutual fund sales and redemptions (excluding money market and limited maturity municipal bond funds). Note that net sales (sales less redemptions) were negative during seven of ten years during the 1970s. In fact, a net outflow of more than $5.7 billion occurred during that decade. So what happened to change the direction? During the early 1980s, two events triggered the acceleration in both gross and net sales. First, interest rates began to top out during mid-1982. Second, one of the most forceful bull markets of the 20th century was unleashed in the fall of 1982.

FIGURE 1.2 □ Ownership of Mutual Funds* Among U.S. Households, 1980-1992 (percent, number of households in millions)

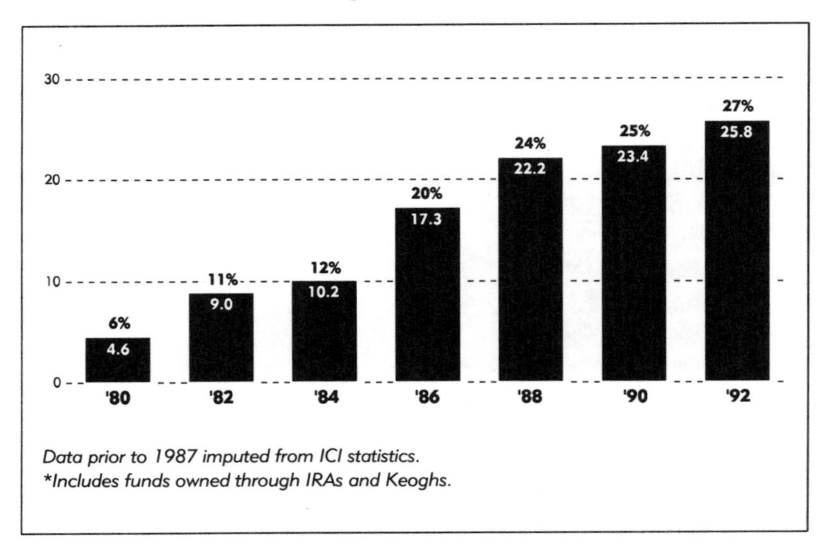

Source: *1994 Mutual Fund Fact Book,* Investment Company Institute, Washington, D.C. Reprinted with permission.

Investors, enticed by the high yields offered by money funds during the late 1970s and early 1980s, began to liquidate their money fund holdings in early 1983 (see Figure 1.3). In fact, investors withdrew more than $40 billion from money market funds during that year. Active marketing efforts by fund groups led to a significant amount of money market mutual fund assets being diverted to equity and bond funds. And from this modest beginning, the rush was on. In 1984, sales of equity, bond and income funds fell a scant $4 billion short of total mutual fund sales during the entire decade of the 1970s! And in 1993, investors purchased more than $500 billion of mutual fund shares. During 1991, 1992 and 1993, mutual fund companies sold more fund shares than they had during their entire 67-year history!

Figure 1.4 depicts the distribution of long-term mutual fund assets. At year-end 1970, the vast majority of mutual fund assets were concentrated in common stocks (80.9 percent). However,

FIGURE 1.3 □ Sales, Redemptions and Assets (billions of dollars)

	EQUITY, BOND & INCOME FUNDS			
Year	**Sales**	**Redemptions**	**Net Sales**	**Assets**
1978	$6.7	$7.2	$(0.5)	$45.0
1979	6.8	8.0	(1.2)	49.0
1980	10.0	8.2	1.8	58.4
1981	9.7	7.5	2.2	55.2
1982	15.7	7.6	8.1	76.9
1983	40.3	14.7	25.6	113.6
1984	45.9	20.0	25.9	137.1
1985	114.3	33.8	80.5	251.7
1986	215.8	67.0	148.8	424.1
1987	190.6	116.2	74.4	453.8
1988	95.3	92.5	2.8	472.3
1989	125.7	91.7	34.0	553.9
1990	149.5	98.2	51.3	568.5
1991	236.6R	116.3R	120.3R	853.0R
1992	364.4R	165.5R	198.9R	1,100.1R
1993	511.6	231.4	280.2	1,510.1

R = Revised

Source: *1994 Mutual Fund Fact Book,* Investment Company Institute, Washington, D.C. Reprinted with permission.

with the introduction of municipal bond funds, the distribution of fund assets among categories of securities began to flatten out. By the end of 1990, less than 40 percent of long-term fund assets were committed to common stocks. This partially explains why mutual fund net sales failed to drop into negative numbers after the stock market crash of 1987, as they did after the 1969–1970 bear market.

Two decades ago, mutual fund investors had virtually only two investment choices—corporate bond funds or common stock funds. But with both bond and common stock prices on the decline during the 1970 recession, investors resorted to a third option. They cashed out of mutual funds and headed for the safe haven that bank savings accounts provided. Because money market funds had yet to be created, mutual fund investors who wanted out of the

FIGURE 1.4 □ Distribution of Mutual Fund Assets

Year	Cash & Equiv.	Corp. Bonds	Pref. Stocks	Common Stocks	Muni. Bonds	Long-Term Gov't. Bonds	Other
1970	6.6%	9.0%	2.4%	80.9%	NA	NA	1.1%
1975	7.6	11.3	1.2	78.6	NA	NA	1.3
1980	9.1	11.3	0.9	71.2	4.9%	2.4%	0.2
1985	8.2	9.9	1.5	47.6	15.2	17.3	0.3
1990	8.5	7.8	0.6	38.1	20.9	22.6	1.5

stock market had little choice but to abandon mutual funds and put their money elsewhere.

Recent Trends in the Mutual Fund Industry

During the past two decades, the mutual fund industry has undergone significant change. Not only have the number and diversity of mutual funds expanded at an astonishing rate; the way funds conduct business has also changed dramatically. The trends described below are more than a historical curiosity. These changes have affected shareholder returns and demand that you scrutinize a fund's characteristics more carefully before making an investment selection. Being aware of the evolving trends in the mutual fund industry could mean the difference between investment success and failure.

Cost of Fund Investing

One of the most important changes in the mutual fund industry in recent years concerns the cost of fund investing. During the 1960s, the vast majority of mutual funds levied front-end sales charges, or *front-end loads.* The loads amounted to 9.3 percent of the amount of money actually invested in the funds. These charges represented commissions, paid primarily to stockbrokers. By the 1970s, *no-load funds*—funds sold by sponsors directly to shareholders without commission—held only about 30 percent of all mutual fund assets. During the late 1970s and early 1980s, however, sales of no-load funds exceeded sales of load funds to the point where the no-load group controlled the majority of fund assets.

SMART STRATEGIES *Be aware of evolving trends in the mutual fund industry. They could mean the difference between your investing success and failure.*

But that trend began to reverse itself with the advent of so-called *12b-1 funds,* which levy annual distribution fees on fund shareholders. A number of existing no-load funds added 12b-1 fees; some front-end load funds dropped their front-end charges and opted instead for a combination of 12b-1 fees and back-end loads. A number of fund families, led by Fidelity, added 2 percent and 3 percent front-end loads to funds that were previously no-load. In addition, brokerage firms, which had previously acted as distributors of mutual funds for other sponsors, launched their own fund families, nearly all of which were loaded with sales charges of some sort. As a result, fewer than one-third of the mutual funds available to individual investors today can truthfully call themselves 100 percent no-load funds.

Load Funds versus No-Load Funds

These days, selecting among funds sold by brokerage firms is a little like searching through alphabet soup. These firms have developed a hub-and-spoke approach to marketing their funds. The hub is the investment portfolio, while the spokes emanating from that hub offer a variety of alternative sales fee payment plans. Class-A shares are sold with a front-end load. Class-B shares are sold without a front-end load. Instead, the investor pays an ongoing 12b-1 charge and a redemption fee when exiting the fund. Some brokerage firms now offer Class-C, Class-D and Class-E shares in addition to the front-end load or redemption-fee options.

Although load funds can and occasionally do outperform no-load funds, when taken in aggregate, no-load funds, on average, outperform load funds by an amount approximately equal to the load. Thus, investors who select from no-load funds have a decided edge over load-fund investors in the long run. Of course, no-load fund investors must do their own homework. However, the extra effort can pay off handsomely. For example, an individual who invests $10,000 annually in no-load funds over a 30-year investment lifetime can pocket $25,500 in commissions that otherwise would go to distributors selling 8.5 percent front-end load funds. Even so-called "modest" 12b-1 charges can mount over an investment lifetime. For example, an individual who invests $10,000 each year in a fund that levies an annual 0.30 percent 12b-1 charge could pay up to $8,000 in distribution fees over a 30-year period.

Management Fees

In addition to sales fees, management fees have risen during the past decade. Twenty years ago, the typical annual management fee amounted to 0.50 percent of fund assets. However, during the 1980s, management contracts of newly organized funds provided for annual adviser fees ranging from 0.75 to 1 percent of fund assets. Although fund assets have swelled during recent years, the average equity fund expense ratio is approximately 1.3 percent. And, of course, higher operating expenses result in lower returns to fund shareholders.

Large Funds versus Small Funds

When mutual funds were swamped with new investor dollars during the 1980s, the net assets of popular funds grew by leaps and bounds. Many modest-sized funds, which sported better than average track records, saw their assets swell into hundreds of millions and even billions of dollars. Although this was a boon to advisers, who earn fees based on the amount of money they manage, shareholders were often shortchanged as fund managers found that they could not produce similar investment results because of the loss of investment flexibility that accompanied the funds' rapid growth. While one can find a few exceptions to the contrary, large funds, on average, tend to underperform smaller funds with similar investment objectives and investment strategies. As a result, beginning in the mid-1980s, a number of popular funds closed their doors to new shareholders.

Portfolio Turnover Ratio

Interestingly, mutual fund portfolio turnover ratios also have risen in recent years. My guess is that competition is the culprit. Most mutual fund investors select their funds based on the funds' recent investment performance. Thus, portfolio managers are forced to attempt to produce short-term returns that exceed those of the market. In trying to do so, these managers jump from one "hot" stock to another. Unfortunately for investors, over the long run, rapid portfolio turnover takes its toll on investment results. Several recent studies have indicated that funds with high portfolio turnover ratios significantly underperform similar funds with low portfolio turnover ratios.

Advertising Abuses

As mutual fund assets grew during the 1980s, so did the Securities and Exchange Commission's (SEC) concern over mutual fund advertising abuses. Knowing that investors' fund selections hung on performance, funds of all kinds began to advertise their "phenomenal" track records. Bond funds advertised double-digit historical annual returns even though the current interest rate environment provided only single-digit yields. Some income funds reported total returns (including capital gains that were pocketed during a falling interest rate environment) rather than yields. GNMA (Government National Mortgage Association, or Ginnie Mae) funds touted their high current yields even though most of their securities were selling above par, and sponsors knew that these returns would eventually erode when homeowners refinanced their existing mortgages at lower interest rates. Equity funds reported their performance for only those periods during which the funds performed well. They completely ignored the times in their history when performance was subpar.

As a result, the SEC adopted a series of regulations governing fund advertising and marketing practices. These rules, explained in more detail in Chapter 2, required income funds to report yields and returns on a similar basis. In addition, any fund that reported its historical return in its advertisements was required to show its performance for ten-year periods rather than arbitrary periods of comparison.

Reporting Requirements

Effected July 1, 1993, amendments to the Investment Company Act have expanded the reporting requirements for most mutual funds. Mutual funds, other than money market funds and index funds, must now disclose the name and title of the person or persons employed by the fund's adviser to be primarily responsible for the day-to-day management of the fund's portfolio. In addition, all funds must include in their prospectuses or annual shareholders' reports a discussion of the factors, strategies and techniques that materially affected the fund's performance. In addition, stock and bond funds now are required to provide a line graph comparing the initial account value and subsequent account values at the end of the most recent ten fiscal years with an "appropriate" broad-based securities market index, assuming a $10,000 initial investment made in both fund and index. These changes continue a trend by fund regulators to require funds to provide substantive communications to both prospective and current fund shareholders.

A Look ahead at Trends To Watch

Given the dramatic events of the past decade, what's in store for the mutual fund industry? First, I believe that the mutual fund industry's explosive growth will moderate considerably over the next several years. Although a number of new funds will come to market in the years ahead, growth will be tempered by consolidation in the industry. A number of small fund families already feel the pinch of increased operating costs and slower sales growth. Some of these fund families will be forced into mergers with larger families, and some will undergo liquidation. Eventually, a few very large players that have the ability and resources to market their wares will dominate the mutual fund industry. Furthermore, consolidation in the brokerage industry will limit the new funds brought to market by this group. While industry assets will continue to expand, I expect the growth in fund assets to outpace the growth in the number of new funds created.

I also expect the trend toward higher costs to continue. Industry sales will be dominated by funds marketed by direct sales forces compensated by expanded sales fees. In addition, administration costs will also continue to rise. Thus, expense ratios will continue to expand. During the past decade, a number of states that had set maximum allowable expense ratios dropped their restrictions. Today, only California retains an expense limitation. However, the state recently raised that limitation from 2 percent of the first $10 million of fund assets to 2.5 percent of the first $30 million.

Note that the Investment Company Act of 1940 has been amended significantly only once (in 1970). This amendment was aimed at curbing the wild abandon of portfolio managers (dubbed gunslingers by the financial press) during the 1960s and at easing the burden of huge sales commissions levied on the initial share purchases of contractual plans. In light of the technological and innovative changes in financial markets since 1970, I expect significant change during the 1990s. At present, the SEC has suggested several changes to the act that would improve the current level of investor protection, facilitate competition and capital formation by removing barriers and encourage innovation in the industry. Here are the major proposals:

1. *Adopt a rule exempting structured financings from the Investment Company Act.* This new proposal would allow mutual funds to invest in bundled credit card receivables, automobile loans and small-business loans that now are prohibited under the act.
2. *Eliminate the exemption from the act of bank collective funds and insurance company separate accounts that hold assets of employee benefits plans.* This proposal would require the sponsors of these asset pools to distribute to participants the same information as do mutual funds (i.e., prospectuses, annual reports, etc.).

3. *Amend the act to permit foreign investment companies to sell shares in the United States.* At present, foreign-based mutual funds must structure themselves as U.S. investment companies, and the SEC must deem it possible to enforce U.S. securities laws before the funds can sell their shares in the United States. Because foreign countries allow different structures than the United States does, this has effectively barred access to the U.S. market.
4. *Amend the act to repeal the retail price requirement.* At present, brokers who sell a load fund's shares must charge fees that conform to those stated in the fund's prospectus. There can be no discounting of fees on a client-by-client basis under current law.
5. *Amend the act to permit the introduction of Unified Fee Investment Companies (UFICs).* These UFICs would charge a fixed percentage of assets to manage and operate a fund. Fund sponsors would profit if costs were less than fees, and investors would profit if costs exceeded fees and sponsors rebated the difference.
6. *Amend the act to allow mutual funds to sell fund shares directly from advertisements.* Currently, fund investors must be sent a prospectus before they invest in a fund. This proposal would allow fund sponsors to sell funds "off the pages" of newspapers and magazines and through the mail. Investors could invest first and receive a prospectus later.
7. *Adopt a rule to permit "limited redemption" investment companies.* This rule would allow funds to redeem shares continuously, but take longer than the mandated seven-day payment. It also would allow fund sponsors to create "interval companies" whose shareholders could redeem their shares at fixed regular intervals such as monthly or quarterly. Today, investors have two investment choices: a closed-end fund that never redeems its shares or an open-end fund that redeems its shares daily. This proposal would allow "half-breed" funds to invest in illiquid securities such as venture capital projects, small-company international stocks and so on without fear that a sudden flood of shareholder redemptions would force portfolio managers to dump their investments at depressed prices.

I believe the discovery of mutual funds by large numbers of investors is one of the big stories of the 1980s. Although investors tend to focus on investment returns when evaluating portfolio management results, reducing investment risk is the single largest benefit that mutual funds provide. Investors, who otherwise might have held highly concentrated portfolios, saw the wisdom of diversification during the turbulent months of late 1987. Although the stock market crash took its toll on the value of mutual fund portfolios, most of the mutual fund investors who rode out the storm now find that their investment wealth is greater than it was before October 1987. And long-term-oriented mutual fund investors will continue to prosper in the years ahead.

2

Exploring the Anatomy of a Mutual Fund

In general, a mutual fund is a financial intermediary that gives individuals the opportunity to pool their capital and invest in a portfolio of securities. Specifically, a *mutual fund* is a corporation chartered by a state to conduct business as an investment company. An *investment company,* in turn, is a financial institution whose sole business and reason for existing is to invest in a portfolio of assets. In general, investment companies are corporations that obtain capital by selling their own securities. They reinvest the proceeds of such sales in a variety of securities issued by governments or corporations. Thus, any income received by investment company shareholders is a function of income from the investment company's portfolio. Furthermore, the price of an investment company's shares is related to the market value of the securities in the company's investment portfolio.

Benefits of Investing in Mutual Funds

The mutual fund industry offers dozens of reasons to invest in mutual funds. Of those, the following are really worth mentioning:

Diversification and reduced risk The greatest benefit of investing in mutual funds is that you instantly achieve a diversified portfolio. To have a chance at winning the investment game, you must be around at the end. The prices of risky individual assets such as common stocks are highly volatile; they can rise and fall by significant amounts in a short period of time. Some stock prices that fall never rise again. But stock prices, when taken in the aggregate (i.e., the market), have always moved to higher ground—even after significant drops over prolonged periods of time. So by buying a mutual fund, you spread your investment risk among a range of assets, not just one, thus reducing your risk.

From the academic community, we have learned that investment risk can be measured in terms of the volatility of investment return. The greater the volatility, the greater the investment risk. Modern investment theory tells us that the risk of a single investment consists of two components: *systematic* (*market-related*) risk and *unsystematic* (*company-specific*) risk. The average common stock, for example, contains 30 percent market risk and 70 percent company-specific risk. That is, 30 percent of the variability in price is related to the ups and downs of the stock market, and 70 percent of the variation in price stems from factors associated with the company. This is an extremely important point, for all of the company-specific (unsystematic) risk can be eliminated with proper portfolio diversification. To state it another way, an individual holding a single stock is subject to three times as much risk as is the well-diversified investor. Therefore, if you cannot hold a well-diversified portfolio of common stocks (or bonds) because of monetary constraints, mutual fund investment is a must.

SMART STRATEGIES *Keep detailed records for each fund. They will save time and help minimize the taxes on your profits.*

Look at it this way: The investor who holds a widely diversified portfolio of common stocks takes only about one-third the risk of an investor who holds a single stock. Because only nondiversifiable, or market-related, risk is rewarded in the stock market, widely diversified investors earn average rates of return nearly equal to investors with highly concentrated portfolios of assets—but do so at one-third the risk.

The average mutual fund, through diversification, reduces the company-specific portion of total risk from 70 percent to only 15 percent. This extreme reduction in investment risk is more than worth the 1 percent or 1.5 percent that we pay portfolio management.

Simplified recordkeeping A second benefit of mutual fund investment is simplified recordkeeping. Anyone who has held 40 or 50 common stocks in a portfolio at a given time knows the trouble caused by scores of dividend checks that, when received, must be cashed and reinvested in additional assets. Also, tracking cash dividend payments, stock splits, interest payments, purchase and sales prices, and brokerage commissions and fees is demanding work. Admittedly, part of the "fun" of investing is cashing dividend and interest checks. However, lost checks can cause aggravation. Additionally, investment returns left in a drawer to collect dust are not nearly as profitable as investment returns reinvested to earn additional returns. Furthermore, at income tax time, the IRS requires that you document all securities trades made during the year, which frequently induces a paperwork nightmare.

With mutual fund investments, management receives and reinvests dividends and interest payments and ultimately pays out this investment income to fund shareholders in a single check. Also, fund investors, through automatic reinvestment plans, can instantly reinvest fund distributions and thus gain the full advantage of compound growth. Finally, every mutual fund shareholder is sent a report once each year that indicates the income earned and transactions made in his or her account during the year. This report can be especially convenient at tax-reporting time.

Liquidity A third benefit of mutual fund investment is that you obtain a high degree of liquidity. That is, it is easy to become fully invested in a diversified portfolio of common stocks (or bonds) in a short period of time. Rather than placing buy (or sell) orders for the scores of stocks that an individually managed portfolio might contain, you can get into or out of the market with a single buy or sell order. Because many funds offer a telephone switch service with a money market fund, you can make a 180-degree turn in investment posture with a single phone call.

Professional management A fourth advantage of fund investment is the presence of low-cost professional management. For a management fee of as little as 0.50 percent, you obtain management governed by a strict investment strategy, as outlined in the fund's prospectus. Thus, to some degree, rationality rather than emotion rules the investment portfolio. Fund managers must stick to the investment objectives outlined in the prospectus.

These professional investment managers work on behalf of shareholders. The fund's adviser (manager) determines the specific securities to be purchased, the timing of such purchases and the proportions of the various asset types the fund holds. Therefore, if you cannot afford to hire professional analysts or portfolio managers, you obtain such guidance at a modest cost because you share mutual fund adviser fees on a pro rata basis with other shareholders. In addition, the fund's adviser bears the cost of data collection, information processing and portfolio tracking. Thus, you can take advantage of modern investment management technology at minimal cost.

Beware of drawbacks On the negative side, I find two disadvantages to mutual fund investment. The first is the relatively high transaction costs fund shareholders incur. While fund managers face lower brokerage commission charges than do individual investors, large block trades widen the spread between a market maker's bid and ask prices, thus raising a fund's total transaction costs.

However, the biggest disadvantage is that, to maintain their conduit status, funds must distribute to shareholders the bulk of the income and capital gains the funds realize during the year. Thus, shareholders possess little control over the tax-planning aspects of their investments. If a fund distributes short-term capital gains to shareholders, the shareholders can do little but pay the taxes (at ordinary income rates) on the gains. While a fund investor can take some precautions to minimize the tax bite, the fact remains that distributions and their tax status are determined by fund management and its portfolio strategies rather than by the needs of fund investors.

The Mutual Fund Family Tree

Let's take a look at how mutual funds fit on the money "family" tree. Figure 2.1 shows the mutual fund's genealogy. As you can see, investment companies encompass three broad subclasses: face-amount certificate companies, unit investment trusts and management companies.

FIGURE 2.1 □ Mutual Fund's Family Tree

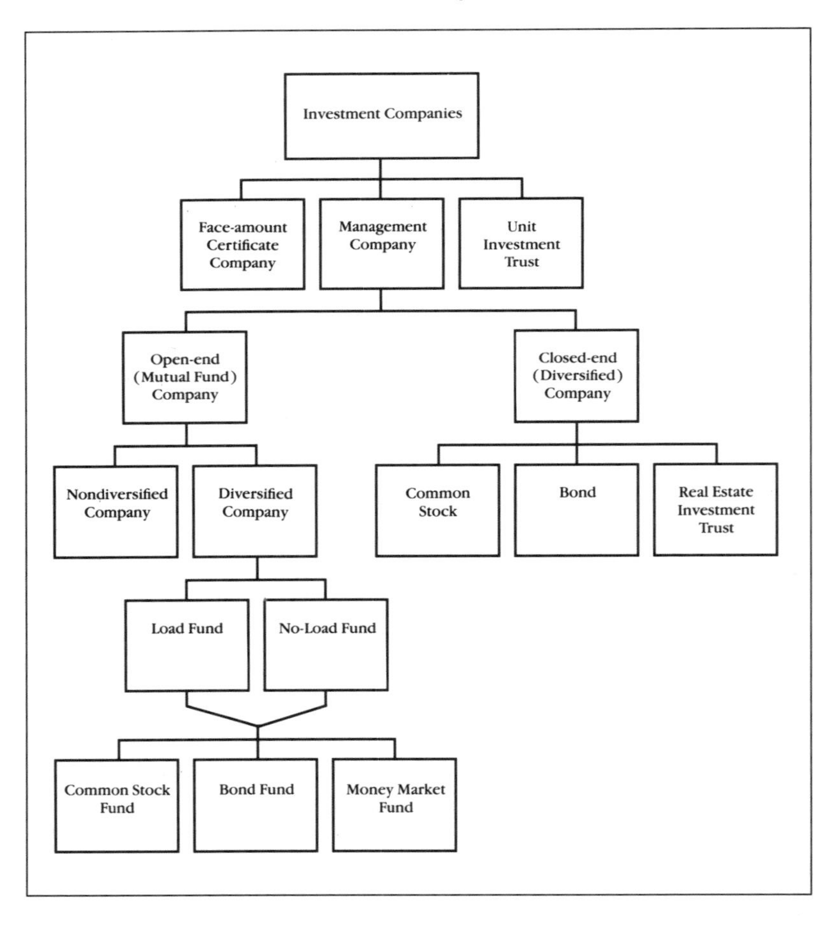

Face-amount certificate companies These companies issue securities that possess a face value payable at the end of an installment period. The principal and interest are guaranteed and usually are collateralized by a specific asset such as real estate. Only a few such investment companies exist today.

Unit investment trusts These are organized under a trust indenture or contract of custodianship that issues redeemable securities, representing an undivided interest in a unit of specific securities. The trust has no board of directors, and because the unit, or pool of assets, is fixed at the outset, the services of a portfolio manager are not needed.

In the 1960s and early 1970s, numerous unit investment trusts were established to give individuals with limited resources an opportunity to invest in diversified portfolios of municipal bonds. (At that time, only unit investment trusts could pass the tax-exempt feature of municipal bonds on to their shareholders.) The trusts were sold with a front-end load (usually from 3 percent to 6 percent), and the proceeds were invested in muni bonds (tax-exempt state and local debt obligations). Interest payments from the investments were passed through to trust participants. The principal amount of the bonds was also returned when the bonds matured. Thus, the trusts were self-liquidating.

While unit investment trust participants benefit from reduced fees because the trust is essentially unmanaged, the lack of management makes the portfolio unresponsive to changing market conditions. Furthermore, unit investment trusts suffer from the absence of a viable secondary market. Trust participants must either hold their certificates until the trust is liquidated or offer large discounts from face value to attract buyers.

Management companies These are the most plentiful members of the investment company family. The management company lineage consists of closed-end investment companies (which include real estate investment trusts, or REITs), nondiversified open-end companies and diversified open-end companies. This last category includes mutual funds available for public purchase and encompasses both load and no-load mutual funds.

Diversified management companies (mutual funds) can be further divided according to the types of securities held. Common stock funds hold primarily common stocks in their investment portfolios. Such funds follow a multitude of portfolio strategies, including aggressive growth, growth, growth and income, and specialty investments (gold funds, etc.). Bond funds generally fall into three classes, including those that hold corporate bonds, U.S. government bonds (including obligations issued by federally sponsored credit agencies) and bonds issued by states and municipalities (munis, or tax-exempt bonds). Money market mutual funds hold securities issued by corporations, banks and the U.S. government that have very short-term maturities. Tax-exempt money market funds are actually muni bond funds that invest in short-term, tax-exempt securities. Thus, they are not really money market funds at all.

How Mutual Funds Are Regulated

The roots of government regulation of investment companies are found in the great stock market crash of 1929, which caused Congress to begin an extensive investigation of the U.S. securities industry. Widespread abuse was uncovered in nearly every segment of the industry. Because of these discoveries, a series of federal statutes was passed aimed at controlling the activities of security issuers, stock exchanges, investment advisers and investment companies. Below are the acts that affect mutual funds.

Securities Act of 1933 Often called the "Truth in Securities Act" or "Disclosure Act," this act attempts to ensure that the investing public has access to adequate information regarding the underlying financial condition of companies offering newly issued securities to individual investors. The act requires that most securities offered for sale in interstate commerce and through the mail be registered with the SEC (Securities and Exchange Commission).

Securities and Exchange Act of 1934 Its objective was to establish and maintain fair and honest markets for securities. This act also designated the SEC as administrator of federal legislation relating to the nation's securities business.

Investment Company Act of 1940 This act contains the bulk of federal powers over the activities of investment companies and provides for the registration and regulation of companies engaged primarily in the business of investing in securities. Below is a summary of the act's major provisions:

- The act provides for registration, "full" disclosure and regulation of investment companies to prevent fraudulent abuses.
- Not more than 60 percent of a fund's board of directors may be affiliated with the fund, its banks or its brokers. (No-load funds need only one outside director.)
- Shareholders and a fund's outside directors must approve management (adviser) contracts.
- A company must redeem shares duly offered by shareholders within seven calendar days at per-share net asset value.
- Open-end companies (mutual funds) may borrow from a bank and use the proceeds for investment purposes (leverage); such debt must be collateralized three to one.
- Mutual funds must send shareholders complete financial reports at least semiannually, and the SEC must see such reports.

Each fund must give a prospectus to prospective investors before sales can be solicited.

The maximum load (commission) cannot exceed 9 percent of the share's offering price.

Either a bank or a broker who is a member of a national securities exchange must keep all securities and cash.

To qualify as a registered diversified management company under the Investment Company Act of 1940, a mutual fund must have at least 75 percent of its assets invested such that (1) not more than 5 percent are invested in any one security issue and (2) not more than 10 percent of the voting securities of any corporation are held by the fund. *Note:* These two conditions refer to only 75 percent of the fund's assets. That is, while 75 percent of the assets of the fund must be diversified, the other 25 percent can be concentrated in a single investment if management desires. However, state *blue-sky* laws (regulations governing the offer and sale of securities) may be more restrictive than those specified in the federal act.

In addition to federal registration, a mutual fund must register in and abide by the laws and regulations of each state in which its shares are sold. In other words, unless a fund is registered in your state of residence, it cannot legally sell its shares to you. Please do not try to purchase fund shares not registered in your state. Most funds maintain a compliance staff to ensure that such purchases are not made. If you use a relative's address instead of your own in an attempt to purchase funds not registered in your home state, you could be in for a legal hassle at some point in the future. What happens if you move to another state after an initial purchase and find out that the fund is not registered in the new state? You'll be able to keep your initial investment in the fund, but will be unable to make further investments. Your best strategy is to find another properly registered fund similar to the one you currently own and make all subsequent purchases in the new fund.

How Mutual Funds Are Managed

The board of directors and officers of a mutual fund carries out the business affairs of the funds. The fund's shareholders actually own the fund; they elect board members and approve various operating policies such as changes in the fund's objective, the hiring of an investment adviser, the adviser's compensation contract, the choice of an auditor and so on.

Fund Adviser/Management Company

The most important task of a fund's board of directors is selecting of the fund's investment adviser. However, because the majority of the board of directors also are principals in a fund management company, it is not surprising that this company is selected as the fund's adviser. (That's why the board started the fund in the first place.) The adviser (or management company) receives a fee for its stock selection and portfolio management activities based on the average value of the assets under management. This fee was traditionally set at approximately 0.5 percent of average fund assets. However, because the costs of doing business continually increase, the fees for newly organized funds tend to be set initially at 0.75 percent to 1 percent of average annual assets.

The management company is responsible for the day-to-day operation of the fund. In a number of cases, the management company (adviser) is responsible for and pays the cost of the following:

- Office space, facilities, personnel and supplies
- Portfolio managers and traders who execute the purchase and sell instructions of the portfolio managers
- Compliance with federal government and state registration regulations
- Preparation and distribution of prospectuses, sales material, advertising, quarterly reports and other shareholder documents
- The transfer of shares purchased or sold by fund shareholders
- Bookkeeping, accounting services, preparation of federal, state and local tax returns and bonding and insurance

Fund Fees

A mutual fund (in other words, you, the shareholder) pays various expenses, including the advisory fee, registration fees, expenses for annual meetings, custodial bank and transfer agent fees, interest and taxes, brokerage commissions, expenses related to the fund's purchases and sales of securities and outside directors' fees and travel expenses. These fees are generally deducted from the fund's dividend and interest income. If income is not sufficient to cover these expenses, fund management can sell some of the fund's assets and use the proceeds to pay expenses. These fees, expressed as a percentage of total assets, are limited by state statute. Expenses exceeding the maximum allowed are reimbursed to the fund by the fund's adviser.

Management/adviser fees A management company profits to the extent that its management fees exceed its cost of doing business. It has been estimated that at a fee of 0.5 percent of total assets, a mutual fund must possess more than $100 million in total assets before the management company becomes profitable. However, before you become too concerned about the welfare of fund managers, recognize that many funds have organized into "families," some of which contain 30 different funds, with billions of dollars under management. Mutual fund management can indeed be lucrative.

Most management companies are also engaged in other businesses closely related to fund management. Thus, the management of mutual fund investor dollars becomes quite a profitable sideline. For example, brokerage firms, life insurance companies and commercial banks have organized most existing front-end load funds. For the most part, no-load funds have been organized by companies engaged in private investment management, including pension fund management.

Generally, the management fee is set on a declining scale relative to fund size. A characteristic fund management agreement follows: "For its services, [the management company] receives a monthly fee of 1/24 of 1% (0.50% annually) of the average daily net assets of the fund up to $250 million. This monthly fee is reduced to 3/80 of 1% (0.45% annually) of the average net assets in excess of $250 million."

In a few instances, the management fee may include an incentive clause. That is, the fee is adjusted upward or downward according to how the fund performs relative to some stock market average or index.

12b-1 fees Beginning in the early 1980s, some mutual funds adopted what has become known as a *12b-1 plan.* The plan is named for the SEC rule that permits such funds to raid the funds' (your) assets to cover their marketing expenses. That is, instead of paying a front-end load to cover marketing expenses, 12b-1 fund investors pay an ongoing charge for marketing. (*Front-end load funds* use the commissions obtained from the load to pay the costs associated with selling new shares.) The SEC 12b-1 rule does not specify the maximum amount of assets that can be appropriated for marketing, and some 12b-1 funds spend more than 0.50 percent of their total assets each year. Over the long run, a payment of this magnitude is much greater than the 4 percent front-end load of funds sold by brokers and financial planners.

Custodians

Can the management of a mutual fund steal the assets and leave the country? If it tries hard enough, it can accomplish anything. However, for mutual funds registered with the SEC, the possibility of losing assets because of theft is quite remote. The Investment Company Act of 1940 requires each registered investment company to establish a custodial relationship with a bank otherwise unconnected with the investment company. The custodial bank holds all the fund's assets (cash and securities) in trust for the fund. The custodian receives the certificates for new acquisitions made by the portfolio manager, pays for securities purchased, delivers securities sold, releases cash to pay fund expenses and accepts dividends and interest payments from the issuers of securities held in the fund's portfolio.

This segment of the securities business is highly specialized. The custodial business of nearly 3,000 registered mutual funds is concentrated in the hands of fewer than 20 banks. Because employees who handle money are bonded by insurance companies, mutual fund shareholders are highly protected against theft.

Transfer Agents

A fund's transfer agent, which may be a bank or some other entity, facilitates the transfer of mutual fund shares (including new purchases and sales), disbursement of dividends and maintenance of shareholder records. Generally, the charges billed to the fund by the transfer agent range from $10 to $12 per account per year.

Distributors and Wholesalers

Distributors and wholesalers represent the sales organization of front-end load funds. The front-end load is the total commission that the investor pays when he or she buys fund shares. The *distributor* of a load fund is generally a separate corporation (usually owned by those with an interest in the fund) that purchases shares from the fund at net asset value (NAV) and sells them to dealers (brokerage firms and large financial planning firms) at NAV plus a commission. *Wholesalers* are agents of the distributor who constantly visit dealers in an attempt to get them to sell fund shares to their customers (you and me).

While a number of front-end load fees begin at approximately 8 percent of the offering price and cannot exceed 9 percent of the offering price by federal law, commission percentages are usually scaled down as the size of a purchase increases. Note that these sales charges are based on the offering amount and not on the amount actually invested (because commissions are taken "up front"). This results in an increase in the percentage of sales fee when related to the amount actually invested. For example, suppose you give $1,000 to a salesperson of a fund with an 8.5 percent front-end load. The 8.5 percent commission ($85) is deducted, and $915 is actually invested in the fund. The effective fee is therefore 85 divided by 915, or 9.3 percent. In other words, the value of the shares purchased must rise by 9.3 percent before you can earn any net investment return. Furthermore, because the sales commission is paid as part of the shares' purchase price, it isn't tax deductible until the shares are sold.

No-load funds are so called because no sales commissions are paid when purchasing their shares. In most instances, a fund's sponsor is also its distributor. Because no-load funds have no sales force or method for compensating brokers, you purchase shares directly from the funds. A no-load fund's share price is identical to its per-share NAV. Thus, 100 percent of your money is invested in no-load fund shares.

What Types of Funds Are Available

In Chapter 3 we will look at the types and characteristics of mutual funds available to individual investors, the returns you can expect and the risks you will face. Here is a brief description of the major categories of funds currently available.

Aggressive growth funds These funds pursue maximum capital gains. They invest aggressively in speculative stocks and tend to stay fully invested over the market cycle. Frequently, these funds use financial leverage (borrowed funds) and may trade listed stock options.

Growth funds The primary objective of growth funds is long-term growth of capital. They generally do not engage in speculative tactics, such as using financial leverage or short-selling. Growth funds tend to be more stable than aggressive growth funds because they usually invest in growth-oriented firms that are older and larger and pay greater cash dividends than the firms sought by aggressive growth funds.

Growth and income funds Generally, such funds invest in common stocks of seasoned, well-established, cash-dividend-paying companies. Portfolio managers attempt to provide shareholders with long-term growth while avoiding excessive fluctuations in NAV.

Balanced funds These funds are generally known as total return funds. Portfolios usually consist of 50 percent high-yielding common stocks and 50 percent bonds and preferred stocks. Balanced funds provide about 50 percent more current yield than the S&P 500 index and are about half as volatile.

International funds Strictly speaking, international funds invest exclusively in foreign securities. However, a number of these funds, called *global funds*, may also invest in U.S. securities.

Asset allocation funds These funds invest across a wide spectrum of assets such as domestic stocks, bonds, gold, international equities, real estate (usually the stocks of REITs) and money market instruments. The goal of such funds is to produce a combination of capital appreciation and current income while reducing risk (share-price volatility).

Precious metals funds These funds invest in gold or silver bullion and the common stocks of gold and silver mining companies. Some of the funds limit their investments to geographical regions (e.g., South Africa or North America), while others invest globally.

Convertible securities funds These funds invest in convertible bonds and convertible preferred stocks. A convertible bond is a debenture that the holder can convert into common stock at his or her option. Thus, when the price of the underlying stock rises, these bonds tend to behave like the stock. However, their value as bonds usually shores up their value during periods of falling stock prices.

Bond funds Designed for income-oriented investors, these funds invest in bonds issued by corporations, the U.S. government, government agencies and state and local governments. Their risk depends on the types of bonds held, their quality and their average maturity.

How To Invest in Mutual Fund Shares

Purchases and sales of open-end mutual fund shares are generally made between you "the investor" and the fund itself. When you purchase fund shares, you make payment to the fund, and the fund issues new shares. When you sell your shares, the fund usually buys them. The fund remits cash to the buyer (using the services of the custodian and transfer agent) and cancels the shares received by the fund. This is called a *redemption.* Thus, most open-end mutual fund purchases are conducted in the primary market rather than the secondary market, in which share price is determined by supply and demand. In a primary market, share price is fixed by the securities issuer.

For no-load mutual funds, share price is equal to a fund's NAV per share. Per-share NAV is determined at the close of each stock exchange business day (usually 4:00 PM New York time) by adding the value of cash and all securities held by the fund, subtracting outstanding liabilities and dividing the result by the number of fund shares outstanding. For example, suppose a fund with 10,000 shares outstanding has determined the value of its securities, cash and liabilities as follows:

Securities value	$100,000
Plus cash	15,000
Total assets	$115,000
Less liabilities	(5,000)
Total net assets	$110,000

NAV of this fund is therefore $110,000 divided by 10,000 shares, or $11. This is the price of any share purchased by no-load fund investors during the period between the previous day's closing value and the value determined at the close of the valuation day. *Note:* If you purchase fund shares during a regular exchange business day, share price would not be known until the close of that day. (This is known as *forward pricing.*) Therefore, any purchase order must be stated in terms of the amount of money you wish to invest in the fund. A redemption order would be stated in terms of the number of shares you wish to sell.

Also worthy of mention is that if this fund sold an additional 1,000 shares at the closing price of $11 per share, the NAV would remain unchanged. The amount of cash the fund holds increases by $11,000 ($11 share price multiplied by 1,000 shares purchased), and total assets increase to $121,000:

Securities value	$100,000
Plus cash	26,000
Total assets	$126,000
Less liabilities	(5,000)
Total net assets	$121,000

When the amount is divided by the 11,000 fund shares now outstanding, NAV per share remains $11. We obtain a similar result when the fund redeems shares.

For mutual fund shares sold with a front-end load, share price is determined by the formula below. If the fund in the previous example were a load fund with an 8 percent sales charge, share price would be $11.96, determined as follows:

$$\frac{\text{Net Asset Value Per Share}}{1-\%\text{ of Commission}}$$

$$\frac{\$11.00}{1-0.08} = \frac{\$11.00}{.92} = \text{Offering Price or } \$11.96$$

Newspapers would report price quotations for the fund's shares at $11 bid and $11.96 ask. *Note:* When purchasing these shares, you obtain an asset worth $11. The difference between the bid and ask prices, 96 cents, goes to the fund's sales organization.

Purchasing Your Fund Shares

When you decide to purchase shares in a fund, you must complete a purchase application, similar to the one required to open a bank account. You mail a check for the amount of purchase along with the application to the fund (if a no-load fund) or give them to the salesperson (if a load fund). At the time you submit the application, you may apply for additional services the fund offers. Such services may include wire transfer privileges, check-writing privileges, telephone exchange privileges and a cash withdrawal plan.

According to federal regulations, all prospective fund investors must receive a prospectus from the fund and declare that they have read it before the fund can accept the application. Before purchase, many investors do not take the time to read the prospectus. These same investors are generally the first to complain when they learn that the fund does not provide certain services or when subsequent purchases or sales of shares are delayed because the shareholder does not understand the procedure for conducting such transactions.

Choosing the Type of Registration

Upon purchase, mutual fund shares must be registered, and you can choose from a variety of ways to do this.

Individual Ownership—shares are registered in your name, giving you sole ownership. Upon your death, they are placed in your estate and disposed of according to the terms of your will.

Joint Tenancy with Right of Survivorship—registration creates joint share ownership. Both you and your joint tenant must sign when redeeming any shares. Shares revert to the sole survivor when one tenant dies.

Joint Tenancy—registration is similar to that described above except that if one tenant dies, the shares go to the estate of the deceased for disposition according to the will. While both tenants live, both must sign for redemptions, and all checks representing fund distributions are made in the names of both.

In addition to these three registration methods, fund shares may be registered with a sole owner (either you or another entity, such as an attorney or a bank) as custodian, as guardian or as a trust under court order.

Recently, the National Conference of Commissioners on Uniform State Laws approved the Uniform Transfer on Death (TOD) Security Registration Act. TOD registration is intended to provide an alternative to the joint tenancy form of title for shareholders who wish to arrange a nonprobate transfer upon their death, but do not wish to share control and ownership during their lifetime.

When you purchase mutual fund shares, the fund will not send stock certificates unless you request it. Instead, ownership is recorded electronically, and the custodial bank keeps a record of the number of shares you buy. Because you can use mutual fund shares as collateral for bank loans (at favorable interest rates), it may be wise to order the fund to send you certificates of ownership periodically. You can store these certificates in a safe-deposit box until you need them. If you order certificates, the fund will deliver them in only whole share amounts. (You can purchase fractions of mutual fund shares.)

Exchanging and Redeeming Shares

Exchanging and redeeming shares are generally as easy as purchasing them. First, if you have telephone exchange privileges, simply call the fund to request an exchange of *X* dollars (or the sale and transfer of *Y* shares) to another fund that qualifies for exchange. Most qualified exchange funds are members of the same fund family (i.e., are managed by the same adviser), although a few funds allow exchanges with nonfamily members. (Remember, the IRS considers any "switch" of fund shares, even among funds in the same family, a taxable event.) When first requesting the telephone exchange privilege, it is wise to make initial purchases of the fund family's money market fund shares. Then you can switch cash by telephone to the desired stock or bond fund. This way, you can make subsequent telephone switches from the stock or bond fund to the money fund, and you can use money fund checks to withdraw cash from the fund family. (This procedure can reduce the time before cash becomes available for use by one to two weeks.)

A second method of selling fund shares is to write directly to the fund and request that shares be sold and the proceeds sent to you. (Remember, while you can request that *some* shares be exchanged by telephone, you cannot close an account [sell *all* shares] unless the fund receives a written and duly signed request to do so.) I suggest that when making a written request, you use a form letter similar to the following:

> Please redeem _______ shares purchased on (date) [or completely liquidate my holdings] in ABC Fund. My account number is ________. Enclosed is certificate number ______ [if certificates are being held by you] for_______shares. Please send the proceeds to (name and address) as soon as possible.
>
> Sincerely,
>
> ______________________________________
>
> Authorized signature(s) Date

To avoid delay in the redemption process, make sure that the signature(s) on the redemption letter have been guaranteed by a bank or a brokerage firm.

The proceeds of share redemptions will be sent as soon as possible. Once the transfer agent (custodial bank) receives your request, it takes an additional one or two days to effect the sale. The custodial bank will then disburse cash within seven days of the sale. Allowing a total of four to six days for mail delivery, expect to receive proceeds from the sale of fund shares within 12 to 15 days after mailing the redemption request. (Remember, also, your bank may not release cash to your account until the fund's check has cleared.) If you wish to reinvest the proceeds in another fund, count on another 3 to 14 days to make the purchase.

Finally, read the fund's prospectus very carefully to determine the extent of all fees associated with the sale and redemption of its shares. Some funds charge a redemption fee if you redeem shares before a specified period of time has elapsed. For example, some funds charge a fee of 0.50 percent of the value of redemption made within 60 days of purchase; others may charge 4 percent on redemptions made within four years of purchase. Most funds levy a flat dollar charge on telephone exchanges that exceed some threshold number during a year. Also, most funds require that initial purchases be on the books for at least 30 days before the funds allow a telephone switch. Remember, a prospectus may be boring to read, but a lack of knowledge regarding your fund's operating procedures will invariably cost you both money and time.

Records You Should Keep

A mutual fund, by law, is obligated to send all shareholders periodic statements of the shareholders' account activity, reports of the fund's investment income and earnings during a period, proxy statements and an updated prospectus. Each fund is also required to submit a semiannual and an audited annual report to shareholders. Some funds voluntarily send unaudited quarterly investment and earnings reports as well. These documents specify the fund's investment portfolio, the income earned during the period and the fund's operating expenses. You must receive a prospectus before the fund can accept your initial share purchases, and the fund will send you a new prospectus each year thereafter.

Keep the latest prospectus on file so you can then buy or sell redemptions according to the fund's latest business procedures. It is also important that you retain all confirmation statements, detailing purchases and redemptions made. At year-end, the fund will send you a summary of the yearly account activity. These statements provide the backup documentation necessary for filing your income tax returns. We suggest that you also keep an account activity summary form similar to the one illustrated in Figure 2.2. It lists the dates of purchases and redemptions, types of transactions, dollar value of each transaction (broken down by the number of shares transacted and the appropriate share price) and a running total of the share balance. Maintain one such document for each fund that you currently own. The reasons for keeping detailed records for each fund you own are to make tax computations easier and to help minimize the federal and state income taxes you pay on mutual fund investment profits. Attach the latest prospectus and all confirmation slips to this summary report.

FIGURE 2.2 □ Mutual Fund Investment Recordkeeping

Name of Fund: Super Growth Shares
Minimum Investment: $1,000
Subsequent Investment: $200
Telephone Number: 1-800-xxx-xxxx
Account Number: xxx-xxx-xxxx
Approximate Distribution Date(s): December

Date	Transaction	Amount	Share Price	Shares	Share Balance
2/28/89	Initial Purchase	$5,000.00	$12.00	416.667	416.667
10/30/90	Purchase	1,000.00	13.00	76.923	493.590
12/30/91	Distribution Sale	422.00	12.90	32.713	526.303
11/14/92	(Redemption)	1,037.46	13.50	76.923	449.380

SMART STRATEGIES *Remember to read the prospectus. Knowing how your fund operates will invariably save you both money and time.*

Several reasons have attracted nearly 30 million U.S. households to mutual fund investing: the benefits are many, the drawbacks are few, and it is easy to track the progress of your investments. In short, mutual funds are ideal vehicles for individuals who wish to expand their wealth. In the following chapters, I'll explain various investment strategies and describe how you can select the best mutual funds to meet your investment needs.

3

Mutual Fund Investing and Taxation

Open-end investment companies that pay out 100 percent of their realized income during the tax year are considered conduits, or pipelines, between their shareholders and the corporations whose securities the funds hold. Thus, all distributions such funds pay create potential tax liabilities for shareholders. This conduit treatment and the fact that mutual funds pay distributions rather than dividends to shareholders usually confuse fund investors and, in some instances, these investors pay federal income taxes that they otherwise could have avoided. The goal of this chapter is to clear up this confusion and perhaps save you a few dollars in the process.

How Mutual Funds (and You) Earn Income

A mutual fund earns income over its tax year by investing in a portfolio of securities and obtaining income in the form of cash dividends and interest paid to the fund by the security issuers. The fund can also earn capital gains income, resulting from price changes of its assets. Such capital gains (or losses) income may be either *realized* (if the fund disposed of securities during the tax year) or *unrealized* (if the fund continues to hold the securities at the end of the tax year). Increases (or decreases) in fund income, whether realized or not, are instantly transmitted to fund shareholders through increases (or decreases) in the value of total assets and thus in the fund's per-share net asset value (NAV).

Shareholders may sell fund shares at any time. At the time of sale, any gains or losses in NAV are realized by the individual shareholder.

Mutual fund shareholders may also realize investment income from the distributions the fund pays. Payments that mutual funds make to shareholders are actually distributions of realized income. On the ex-distribution date, the fund's per-share NAV will fall by the amount of that distribution. Thus, the income you receive from the distribution is offset exactly by the decrease in NAV. For example, suppose that a fund with a $10 NAV plans to distribute $.25 to its shareholders. On the ex-distribution date, the fund pays $.25 per share cash distribution and the NAV of the fund falls to $9.75. Because shareholders realize the income distributed to them and are taxed accordingly, the fund must indicate the source of the components of all distributions paid during the year. The various components and their tax treatments are discussed below.

Net investment income This is the income a fund earns from cash dividends and the interest payments it receives less management fees and fund operating expenses. This income is considered to be ordinary income and is thus taxed at the taxpayer's marginal rate.

Capital gains income In trading securities, a fund may realize capital gains and losses. The realized capital gains and realized capital losses are netted, and the excess realized capital gains are paid out to shareholders. If the difference between realized capital gains and realized capital losses results in a net loss, the fund is allowed to carry the loss forward. These capital losses can be used to offset net realized capital gains in future periods.

Because each mutual fund cash distribution results in an immediate decline in per-share NAV equal to the distribution amount, individuals who purchase mutual fund shares immediately before the ex-distribution date effectively have a portion of their investment capital returned to them. The distribution is considered a taxable event, and even though the distribution equals the decrease in NAV, investors are left worse off by the amount of tax they must pay on the distribution.

For example, suppose you invest in a fund one day before its ex-distribution date. On the ex-distribution date, the fund distributes a large capital gain, and the fund's share price falls by an amount equal to the distribution. If you have taken the dividend reinvestment option, you will end up that day with more shares trading at a lower price. The value of your initial investment will stay the same because all distributions are reinvested in additional shares. However, that distribution is a taxable event, and you must ante up an amount equal to 28 percent of the capital distribution, even though you are just getting a return of your initial investment.

The rub is that you won't know the size of the capital distribution until it is paid. Your fund will not tell you what that distribution will be because it probably won't know until a final tally is made near year-end. Although many fund managers attempt to sell losing positions near year-end to balance gains taken earlier in the year, whenever the stock market stages a prolonged rally to the upside, most equity funds do not possess enough losing positions to reduce their gains. The result can be a hefty capital distribution and a large and unexpected tax bill.

So what can you do? Keep an eye out for a few telltale signs before making an investment in a fund near year-end. First, if the fund has a high portfolio turnover ratio and a decent return for the year, most likely that fund will be forced to pay a hefty distribution in December. On the other hand, new funds with low portfolio turnover ratios can usually avoid paying large capital distributions. Funds that have recently performed poorly usually have plenty of losses to balance gains. For example, most gold funds returned more than 80 percent in 1993, but losses that piled up during the previous five years enabled most precious metals funds to avoid large capital distributions at the end of the year.

Check a fund's latest annual or semiannual shareholder report. These reports list unrealized gains and losses. Postpone until shortly after the ex-distribution date an intended investment in any fund with a large net unrealized gain position that could signal a high potential tax liability. Remember, those gains were earned by someone else.

If a fund surprises you with a hefty capital gains distribution before year-end, dump that fund immediately. Your realized loss (caused by the fall in the fund's share price as a result of the distribution) will offset the realized capital gains distribution. Reinvest the proceeds in another fund with a similar objective and investment style. Remember, the amount of money you earn is not always the gauge of investment success; sometimes it's what you get to keep that really matters.

The Tax Advantage of Losses

Because mutual funds can carry forward their net realized capital losses, it is possible for new investors to "buy" the tax advantage of losses suffered by others. First, I must point out that, whenever possible, mutual fund managers try not to distribute capital gains to shareholders; yet they cannot risk endangering their conduit status. They recognize that shareholders prefer gains in per-share NAV (rather than distributed capital gains) because unrealized capital appreciation goes untaxed while capital gains distributions are subject to shareholder federal income taxes in the year distributed. Thus, as year-end approaches, managers with net realized capital gains positions begin to sell off assets that have declined in value and apply realized capital losses carried forward from prior periods until total realized losses equal total realized gains. This gimmick eliminates bothersome taxable capital distributions. The following example shows you the advantage of buying a fund with realized capital losses that are carried forward.

SMART STRATEGIES *If a fund surprises you with a hefty capital gains distribution before year-end, dump that fund immediately. Your realized loss will offset the realized capital gains distribution. Reinvest the proceeds in another fund with a similar objective and investment style.*

Example: Suppose two mutual funds currently own exactly the same assets. Both are no-load funds with NAVs equal to $10. Fund X purchased its portfolio of securities at about one-half of today's market value; therefore, the fund has a net unrealized capital gains position. Fund Y acquired the securities in its portfolio recently, after liquidating assets that had declined in value over the preceding year; thus, it has net realized capital losses to carry forward. Because both funds hold exactly the same securities, Fund Y is a more desirable investment than Fund X. To see why, consider what would happen if the assets held by both funds rise in price. If Fund Y sells some of its holdings, it can use the losses carried forward to offset the realized gains. If Fund X sells some of its securities, a distribution of capital gains must be made because the fund is left with a net realized capital gains position (it has more capital gains than losses). The fund's shares will fall in price by an amount equal to the distribution, but Fund X shareholders are at a disadvantage, compared to those holding Fund Y's shares, by the amount of personal taxes they must pay on the distribution.

Identifying Gains and Losses

As I have stressed, it is very important that you maintain adequate records of all your share purchases, *including* shares purchased through reinvestment of distributions and redemptions. In addition to a summary report of fund purchase and sale transactions, keep all statements from the fund that document specific purchases and sales.

When fund shares are sold (redeemed), you may realize a profit (or loss). The amount of profit (or loss) is determined by the difference between the price at redemption and the cost basis. If no records of prior purchases exist, it may be virtually impossible to determine or substantiate the magnitude of the gain or loss.

FIFO and Identifiable Cost Methods

For income tax purposes, the cost of mutual fund shares that have subsequently been sold can be determined by either the *first in, first out* (FIFO) method or by the *identifiable cost* method. The

FIFO method assumes that the shares sold were the first ones acquired. The identifiable cost method requires that the shares sold be specifically identified as the ones acquired on a specific date at a specific acquisition cost.

When you use the identifiable cost method of accounting for share costs, the IRS places the burden of proof on you, the taxpayer. That is, you must be able to trace a sale to a specific block of shares. The easiest way to do that is to request, periodically, that your fund send you stock certificates that represent your holdings. When a sale is made, record the certificate number(s) and the date of acquisition, along with the original cost and proceeds received. If you leave your shares on deposit with the fund (as most fund investors do), keep a record of each purchase made. When a sale is made, write to the fund and instruct it to sell a specific block of shares acquired on a specific date. Request that the fund verify the sale in writing.

Remember also that, when you liquidate your holdings, you may have acquired shares through automatic reinvestment of distributions. Thus, the cost basis for these shares is the per-share NAV at the time of reinvestment. Because the income tax liability on these shares may have been partially satisfied in prior years, ignoring the cost of shares acquired this way could result in overpaying your income taxes.

Example: Suppose you invested $2,000 in Fund XYZ two years ago. Because the NAV at that time was $10, you acquired 200 shares. Recently, you liquidated your holdings in this fund and received $3,000. It might appear that you owe taxes on $1,000 of realized capital gains. However, suppose the fund made distributions during this period totaling $600. Because these distributions were taxed previously, the investment income subject to taxation at the time of liquidation is $400, not $1,000. Thus, I cannot overstate the need to maintain good mutual fund accounting records.

4

Choosing the Right Type of Fund for You

Although the incredible expansion in the number of mutual funds has made selecting mutual funds much more complex, the proliferation of funds has had a great side benefit. The diversity of funds now available has given individual investors the opportunity to assemble portfolios with risk and return characteristics never before available. In fact, you—as an individual investor—can now engage in portfolio management tactics formerly reserved for only the largest corporate and public pension funds. Because investing in a fund is like hiring your own personal portfolio manager, you can now assess your investment objectives, establish risk and return parameters, and outline the strategies you would like your portfolio manager to implement. You then can begin searching for the funds that meet these specific requirements. After that, you can monitor the progress of each portfolio manager (fund) and relate its performance to others with similar investment objectives, strategies and styles. You can "fire" a manager with suboptimal performance by selling that fund and then "hiring" another manager whose recent performance more closely conforms to your requirements.

Today, you can most likely find a mutual fund that invests in the categories of assets you desire, possesses the strategy you demand and operates in the style you prefer. (See Figure 4.1.) That's something that could not be said a few years ago. However, before searching for the best funds, you need to know the categories of funds currently available and the risk and return characteristics of these categories of funds. The pages that follow describe the various general categories of funds and outline the strategies that groups of funds within each category use.

Aggressive Growth Funds

Aggressive growth funds pursue as their primary investment objective maximum capital gains. They invest aggressively in speculative stocks and tend to stay fully invested at all times. Some funds in this category use financial leverage (that is, borrow additional capital on margin to increase their equity exposure and enhance returns), others invest in the stocks of small growth companies (i.e., small-cap stocks), while others attempt to purchase common stocks of the fastest growing companies regardless of

FIGURE 4.1 □ Mutual Fund Financial Statistics (Medians)

Category	Return 1993	Return 5 Yr.	Current Yield	Beta	Turnover Ratio	Expense Ratio
Aggressive Growth	16.2%	113%	0.0%	1.14	70%	1.29%
Growth	10.8	92	0.7	1.00	56	1.25
Growth and Income	11.3	82	2.4	0.78	50	1.43
International Stock	34.2	60	0.3	0.56	55	1.75
Precious Metals	78.1	43	0.1	–0.26	53	1.88
Corporate Bond	9.8	64	—	—	74	0.80
Government Bond	8.0	60	—	—	97	0.80
Municipal Bond	12.3	58	—	—	28	0.71

whether they are large or small. Some aggressive growth funds invest in highly concentrated portfolios, consisting of stocks in a handful of industries. Others attempt to enhance their returns by investing in stock market derivatives such as puts and calls.

Needless to say, the share prices of aggressive growth funds tend to be highly volatile, performing very well during bull stock markets and faring very poorly during stock market corrections or long bear stock markets. On average, funds in this category possess *betas* that average about 1.15 (that is, they are about 15 percent more volatile that the stock market as a whole), and a number of aggressive growth funds possess betas of 1.40 or more. (Beta is an index of portfolio volatility. The stock market possesses a beta of 1.00. A fund with a beta of 1.40 is 40 percent more volatile than the market.) Thus, investment in these funds is not for the faint of heart. Generally, aggressive growth funds are not appropriate for conservative investors unless they form a small portion of a highly diversified portfolio. On the other hand, these funds are suitable investments for long-term investors who can assume above-average risks and are not bothered by short-term stock market fluctuations. However, over the long run, because of the additional risks aggressive growth funds assume, most are capable of delivering above-average investment returns. Over a ten-year period, for example, aggressive growth funds should return an average of about 200 basis points per year more than the overall stock market. In other words, if you seek average annual returns in the range of 10 percent to 20 percent, look no further than the category of aggressive growth equity funds.

Growth Funds

As this name implies, growth funds attempt to obtain long-term growth of investment capital as their primary investment objective. The portfolio managers of these funds do not engage in speculative tactics such as using financial leverage, concentrating their portfolios in a handful of stocks drawn from a few industries or using short-selling tactics. However, on occasion, some managers will use stock or index options to hedge their portfolios. That is, they purchase puts in an attempt to cushion the blow that can be delivered during a sharp and swift stock market correction. (A *put* option gives the holder the right to sell a stock or market index at a specified price for a limited period of time. If the price of the underlying security declines, the holder can "put" (sell) the security to the option writer at a price above its current market price.)

The returns of growth funds tend to be less variable than those of aggressive growth funds. On average, these funds possess betas of 1.00 (that is, they offer a level of risk equal to that of the stock market as a whole). In addition, because growth funds tend to invest in the common stocks of larger, more established companies that usually pay cash dividends, this group of funds also provides a modest amount of current income. You are likely to find the stocks of highly visible firms such as AT&T, Ford, Xerox and DuPont in the typical growth fund's portfolio. Although a handful of growth funds attempt to boost returns by engaging in market timing tactics, the vast majority of funds in this category tend to stay fully invested at all times. Furthermore, growth fund portfolio managers often hold their investments in blue chip stocks for a longer period than do managers of more speculative funds. The average turnover ratio (an index of the fund's security trading activity) for growth funds averages about 60 percent versus an average of more than 80 percent for other categories of equity funds.

A large percentage of funds in the growth category have operated for decades. Many of these funds are household names. In addition to actively managed funds, you can find a number of index funds in this category. These funds attempt to duplicate the performance of the stock market by constructing portfolios that replicate popular stock market indexes such as the Standard & Poor's 500 index or the Dow Jones Industrial Average. Although it is true that you can't beat the market if you own it, index funds generally have relatively low expense ratios and portfolio turnover rates. Thus, these low-cost funds ensure delivery of nearly the full measure of the stock market's long-term return.

Over long periods of time, growth funds tend to return annually about 6 percent to 7 percent more than the rate of inflation. Historically, these funds have provided long-term annual returns that average from 10 percent to 12 percent. Considering the cost of investing, growth funds have attained an enviable record of meeting their mandated investment objective of long-term growth of capital.

Growth and Income Funds

Growth and income funds seek a high level of current income, some capital appreciation and the preservation of capital. This category includes balanced funds and equity income funds.

Balanced funds (generally referred to as *total return* funds these days) invest in portfolios of common stocks and bonds. The allocation either may be fixed by investment policy or may vary, depending on the category of assets a fund's portfolio manager believes will perform best in the near future. Some balanced funds invest in convertible bonds and preferred stocks. Given the allocation between both stocks and bonds, growth and income funds tend to possess relatively low betas (most range from 0.40 to 0.60). This implies that they are far less volatile than the stock market as a whole. While this tends to be true, under some circumstances, growth and income funds can exhibit extreme volatility. While they provide some protection during periods of declining stock prices, they are highly interest rate sensitive, and their share prices can decline by significant amounts during periods of rising interest rates and falling stock prices. Thus, at times, they can be more risky than most conservative investors believe.

Equity income funds invest primarily in common stocks that have higher dividend yields than the dividend yield of the Standard & Poor's 500 index (a commonly accepted proxy for the U.S. stock market). These are usually the stocks of highly visible, multibillion dollar companies with long operating histories. In addition, the common stocks held by equity income funds tend to have relatively low betas, lower-than-average price-earnings ratios and relatively low price-to-book value ratios. These are the stocks preferred by so-called value investors. Because of their generous dividend yields, you can usually find a number of stocks of public utilities and financial companies (for example, banks, savings and loans, and insurance companies) in an equity income fund's portfolio. As a consequence, the per-share net asset values (NAVs) of these funds tend to fall less than the overall stock market during a correction or bear market. However, they also rise less than the typical growth fund's NAV during bull markets.

Growth and income funds tend to suit for conservative investors who will not assume the full measure of risk associated with equity investments. Because of their "value" bent, these funds tend to be less volatile than the stock market, and they frequently possess generous current yields. Thus, investors who want current income may find growth and income funds suitable additions to their overall portfolios. Although these funds' current dividend yields tend to be less than those of income funds such as bond funds, their long-term total returns are often greater than those obtained from the typical bond fund because growth and income fund managers allocate a significant portion of their assets to common stocks. In other words, these funds offer income investors a degree of inflation protection that is not present in a pure fixed-income fund. As a consequence, not only do these funds suit for conservative growth-oriented investors, they suit for the portfolios of income investors because of the funds' inflation offset.

International Funds

In recent years, international funds have been one of the fastest growing segments of the mutual fund industry, and with good reason. The rise of capitalism in the former Soviet Union, the need for infrastructure and modern production facilities in China, the privatization of state-owned companies in Latin America and the North American Free Trade Agreement have created significant investment opportunities all over the world. Today, stock markets located outside the United States account for nearly two-thirds of the market value of all publicly traded stocks, and that share of stock market trading will surely increase before the turn of the century. In short, it is naive to assume that the best investments can be found only in the United States.

International funds can be divided into five groups:

1. *Global funds* invest in both U.S. and foreign securities.
2. *Diversified international funds* restrict their security holdings to companies domiciled outside the United States.

3. *Regional funds* invest in countries in a specific geographic area, such as Europe, Latin America or the Pacific Basin.
4. *Country-specific funds* limit their investments to issuers domiciled in a single country.
5. *Specialty funds* concentrate their portfolios in specific industries, such as global telecommunications, or in specific categories of international equities, such as small-firm stocks or the stocks of companies in emerging markets.

Investment risk tends to parallel a fund's degree of diversification, with the most diversified (global funds) possessing the least risk and the most concentrated (single-country funds) possessing the greatest degree of price volatility. In general, international equity funds tend to be riskier than domestic equity funds. First, international equity funds expose their shareholders to business and economic risks similar to those assumed by shareholders of domestic equity funds. In addition, U.S. investors holding foreign stocks are subject to political and foreign exchange risks. Political risks arise because those who invest money outside U.S. borders have no guarantee that it will return. Investors holding Tsarist bonds or shares of stock in Cuban companies need not be told of the risk that a change in government can introduce. Furthermore, a degree of price volatility exists because of changing rates of exchange among the U.S. dollar and major foreign currencies. That is, when the value of the dollar rises, returns from international securities (restated in dollar terms) tend to fall. On the other hand, when the value of the dollar falls, the returns of international securities are often enhanced. Thus, the total risk of an international equity fund suffers from the compound effects of business, economic, political and foreign exchange risks.

Although international equity funds often contain more risk than their domestic counterparts, you have two compelling reasons to consider including one or two quality international equity funds in your overall portfolio. First, economic growth in some regions of the world is much stronger than it is in the United States. For example, during the last couple of decades, China's gross domestic product (GDP) has grown at a 10 percent real annual rate versus the slightly less than 3 percent annual rate for the United States and most European industrialized economies. And countries with greater-than-average economic growth rates provide exceptional growth opportunities for corporate investors. In addition, the returns from foreign securities tend to have relatively low degrees of correlation with returns from U.S. securities. Thus, a portfolio consisting of both domestic and foreign stocks tends to possess less volatility or investment risk than a portfolio whose assets are concentrated in a single country. In fact, numerous academic studies indicate that an optimally balanced equity portfolio is one in which one-third to one-half of its assets are allocated to foreign stocks. This mix, according to the studies, delivers the greatest return for the least amount of volatility or investment risk.

SMART STRATEGIES *Include one or two international equity funds in your portfolio, because growth is stronger in some parts of the world than in the United states and because of the low correlation of return between U.S. and foreign stocks.*

Because of the relatively low correlation of returns between foreign and domestic stocks, international funds tend to possess relatively low betas (on average, about 0.60). However, as discussed above, these funds possess greater-than-average risk, which the beta statistic does not reflect completely. In addition, international equity funds generally possess very low dividend yields. Finally, because most international funds channel their investments to many different countries, U.S. investors are subject to a wide variety of tax laws. Unlike the conduit tax treatment afforded domestic funds, funds that diversify internationally must pay foreign income taxes on income received from investing in a host of countries. These tax payments are reported to international fund shareholders once each year because the payments can be used as credits against U.S. income tax liabilities. However, documenting these tax payments on your U.S. tax return can sometimes create a paperwork nightmare.

Taken by themselves, international equity funds can be quite risky. Thus, they are not suitable as a complete investment program. However, given their low correlation of returns with domestic securities, they possess substantial opportunities to decrease overall portfolio risk. When taken as part of a complete investment program, therefore, international equity funds can be suitable investments for both conservative and aggressive growth-oriented investors.

Sector Funds

Sector funds invest in very concentrated portfolios of common stocks, usually drawing their selections from a single industry. Although most sector funds got their start during the past decade, this investment strategy is not new to the mutual fund industry. For example, Century Shares Trust, which invests the vast majority of its assets in insurance stocks, began operations in 1931. However, the floodgates to sector investing opened in 1981 when Fidelity Management and Research initiated the Fidelity Select Portfolios Fund, which initially gave investors the opportunity to concentrate in, and switch between, one or more of the following industries: technology, utilities, health care, energy, precious metals and financial services. (During the next decade, Fidelity expanded the number of sectors in its Select Portfolios to more than three dozen.) Invesco (formerly Financial Programs) and Vanguard shortly followed suit, establishing funds with similar industry portfolios.

Except for distributors of sector funds of popular growth industries such as technology and health care, high-yielding industries like utilities and financial services, and those that provide an inflation hedge—energy, for example—mutual fund distributors have had difficulty attracting large numbers of investors to industry-concentrated funds in recent years. Thus, little expansion has occurred in the number of sector funds during the last few years. In fact, a number of sector funds have merged during the past couple of years because of their inability to attract a large following among mutual fund investors. And for good reason.

One of the greatest benefits of investing in mutual funds is the risk reduction that investors receive by holding a highly diversified portfolio of common stocks. On average, the typical diversified common stock fund contains one-third the risk contained in a portfolio consisting of a single stock. Industry-concentrated portfolios, on the other hand, contain significantly more risk than the typical equity fund. That's because the economic factors that affect a single company in an industry tend to impact all companies in that industry. For example, bank stocks tend to rise during periods of declining interest rates and fall during periods of increasing interest rates because their profit margins expand and contract when interest rates fluctuate. Thus, when interest rates rise and bank profit margins shrink, the prices of all bank stocks often decline. In short, the share prices of sector funds tend to be highly volatile. Each year, a handful of sector funds surge to the top of the performance chart, and a handful get mired at the bottom.

SMART STRATEGIES *Because of their highly concentrated assets and their extreme volatility, sector funds are not for the faint of heart. Investors should approach this category of funds with extreme caution.*

Sector funds seem to appeal to three types of investors. Investors who seek above-average current yields from their equity portfolios often gravitate toward utility, bank or insurance stocks. Rather than putting all of their "eggs" (in this case, investment nest eggs) in one basket, they attempt to distribute them among many baskets by investing in high-yielding sector funds. Some aggressive investors seek to increase their long-term returns by investing a portion of their assets in the stocks of one or two high-growth industries such as telecommunications or technology. Finally, some investors try to make the most of the business cycle by practicing what is known as *sector rotation.* Sector rotation is an attempt to continually reallocate assets among industries that are affected differently by changes in the business cycle—for example, investing in interest-rate-sensitive industries during an economic downturn, cyclical stocks during the early stages of an economic turnaround and consumer stocks during a period of robust economic growth.

Because of their highly concentrated assets and their extreme volatility, sector funds are not for the faint of heart. Investors should approach this category of funds with extreme caution.

Precious Metals Funds

More than three dozen mutual funds provide investors with access to the precious metals markets. Some of the funds invest in gold bullion and the shares of gold mining companies only; others expand their portfolios to include investments in silver and platinum. A few funds restrict their investments to specific geographical areas such as South Africa or North America.

On balance, the NAVs of precious metals funds are often much more volatile than the underlying prices of gold and silver bullion. That's because most precious metals funds invest heavily in mining stocks, whose earnings and share prices tend to be highly variable because they operate in a high-fixed-cost industry. For example, suppose that the annual cost to extract 600,000 ounces of gold from a mine is $200 million. When the price of gold is $360 an ounce, revenues amount to $216 million, and operating profits total $16 million. Now suppose the price of gold rises 20 percent to $432 an ounce. Revenues increase to $259 million and, because operating costs are unaffected, operating profits rise by 270 percent to $59 million.

The price of gold is driven by one basic force: fear (or the lack of it). Political instability, the prospect of an increasing rate of inflation and the falling value of the dollar tend to drive the price of gold higher. Thus, the return from investing in a precious metals fund usually fluctuates inversely with the returns of most other categories of financial assets. As a result, investment in gold tends to lower portfolio volatility when coupled with investment in stocks and bonds. In other words, gold funds provide an excellent hedge for both growth-oriented and income-oriented investors who have packed their portfolios with either equity or bond funds. However, because many precious metals funds invest in gold mining shares of companies doing business outside the United States, these funds are exposed to both political and foreign exchange risk.

Interestingly, gold has proved to be an excellent hedge against inflation (or inflation fears) for centuries. However, over long periods of time, the price of gold bullion has advanced at a rate just about equal to that of the rate of inflation. In other words, a long-term commitment to a well-managed gold fund will provide an average annual rate of return approximately equal to that of Treasury bills or money market mutual funds. Thus, a large allocation to gold funds maintained over long periods of time will depress portfolio returns. Considering the extreme share price volatility that these funds exhibit, you have better places to invest your capital. On the other hand, during short periods of time, gold funds can produce handsome returns. For example, during 1993, when inflation fears ran rampant, the Lexington Strategic Investments Fund returned a whopping 270 percent!

Asset Allocation Funds

Asset allocation has become a modern-day financial buzzword. It describes portfolios that contain two or more classes of assets. Even some market timers who switch their investments back and forth between stocks and cash refer to themselves as asset allocators. However, to me, true asset allocators are those who spread their investments among several asset categories whose returns are less than perfectly correlated with one another, such as domestic stocks, international stocks, bonds, precious metals and so on. Thus, the objective of the true asset allocator is to produce meaningful returns while minimizing investment risk.

Asset allocation funds differ greatly. Some include securities from only two or three asset categories in their portfolios. Others expand the list of categories to a half-dozen or more. Some asset allocation funds, such as the Merriman Asset Allocation Fund, invest exclusively in other mutual funds. Still other funds, such as the Vanguard Star Fund, invest exclusively in mutual funds that are members of the funds' own families.

When guiding their asset allocation funds, some portfolio managers apply a passive reallocation strategy, such as rebalancing the portfolios back to their initial allocations once each quarter. Others attempt to forecast returns in the various categories in which they invest—an active reallocation strategy. They then reallocate the funds' assets, giving more weight to those asset categories that they expect to produce the best returns. Thus, when investing in an asset allocation fund, it is very important to know which classes of assets the fund invests in as well as whether management follows a passive or an active reallocation strategy.

In theory, asset allocation funds should provide greater rates of return than the stock market as a whole, but offer less volatility. Unfortunately, asset allocation funds are somewhat new additions to the investment world (the grandfather of asset allocation funds, the Permanent Portfolio Fund, began operations during 1982). Thus, we have insufficient data to judge how investment fact will measure up to investment theory.

Since making their debut in the early 1980s, asset allocation funds have underperformed the Standard & Poor's 500 index, which is packed with blue chip stocks. But before summarily dismissing the concept of asset allocation, you must remember that these funds usually shine during periods marked by financial adversity. Their return comparisons pale, however, when blue chip stocks perform well, consumer prices grow at modest rates and interest rates remain relatively stable. These are precisely the conditions that have prevailed in the financial markets since asset allocation funds appeared. Thus, it is not surprising that the returns from asset allocation funds have been relatively unimpressive when compared to the performance of common stocks.

It is also not fair to compare the returns of asset allocation funds with those of popular stock market indexes. Most asset allocation funds invest in bonds, cash equivalents and other assets such as gold and precious metals. As a result, they tend to possess far less risk than the typical equity fund. In fact, the average beta of funds in this category is about one-half that of the typical equity mutual fund. Thus, asset allocation funds are ideally suited for conservative, growth-oriented investors because they possess relatively low risk, provide a modest current yield and are capable of producing double-digit returns over longer periods of time.

Convertible Bond Funds

A *convertible* is a corporate bond that, at the holder's option, can be exchanged for shares of the issuer's common stock. When the price of a company's common stock rises above the bond's *conversion price* (found by dividing the par value of the bond—that is, its stated or face value—by the number of shares of common stock into which it can be converted), the bond's price tends to move in tandem with the underlying stock's price. On the other hand, because these securities also pay interest and have limited lives, their prices often behave like bond prices when the common stock price falls below the conversion price. Thus, a portfolio of convertible bonds allows investors to participate in rising stock markets while giving them a degree of protection during severe bear stock markets.

Although investment in convertible bonds at first glance appears to be the ideal investment strategy for conservative, growth-oriented investors, implementing a convertible bond strategy does not come without pitfalls. The convertible bond market is relatively small and thinly traded. Thus, trading costs tend to be high. In addition, the prices of convertible bonds can sink when rising interest rates cause a bear stock market. First, the bonds lose value because their underlying stocks lose value. Second, their value decreases along with other bond values in an environment of rising interest rates.

Convertible bond funds differ significantly from each other with respect to how greatly they stress fixed-income and equity characteristics. In varying degrees, most convertible bond funds blend the pursuits of growth and income. But some funds go to extremes, greatly prioritizing one over the other. A fund's potential risks are directly proportionate to the degree to which the fund stresses growth over income.

You can gain much insight into a convertible bond fund's objectives by looking at its income stream. Generally, the greater a fund's yield, the more it stresses income and price stability at the expense of potential capital gains. Bolder vehicles that aggressively pursue growth lie at the opposite end of the spectrum. These convertible bond funds tend to invest heavily in securities of emerging-growth companies and stress high-growth industries such as technology and pollution control. The majority of convertible bond funds, however, fall somewhere between these two extremes.

Convertible bond funds tend to possess far less volatility than the stock market as a whole, with an average beta of 0.60. Although their current yields are usually less than those of bond funds, they provide far greater yields than are available in the stock market. As you could expect, convertible bond funds often deliver exceptional returns when interest rates decline and stock prices rise.

Taxable Bond Funds

At the beginning of the 1980s, fewer than 120 bond funds of all types existed. By the decade's end, that number had swelled to more than 1,700. Today you can choose from more than 2,000 bond and income funds. During that decade of hectic growth, several categories of specialized bond funds emerged, including Ginnie Mae funds, government income funds, international bond funds and municipal bond funds that concentrate their investments in the issues of a single state. In addition, a growing number of funds now target their maturities by investing in zero-coupon bonds with specific maturity dates. You also now can invest in renegotiable-rate home mortgages, which dominate the portfolios of ARM (adjustable-rate mortgage) funds. Thus, today's income-oriented investor can find bond funds that assume a wide spectrum of risks in their pursuit of current income.

U.S. government income funds invest in a variety of government securities, including Treasury bonds, federally guaranteed mortgaged-backed securities and issues of government agencies such as the Federal Home Loan Bank System, Federal Farm Credit, Student Loan Marketing and the Tennessee Valley Authority. These bonds pay interest that is taxable at the federal level, but not at the state and local levels. U.S. government bond fund shareholders receive a pass-through of the exemption from state and local taxes on interest income earned. The portfolio managers of some government bond funds attempt to enhance returns by investing in financial derivatives, a strategy that can add significant risk to an otherwise modest risk bond portfolio.

GNMA funds (Government National Mortgage Association, or *Ginnie Mae*) invest in government-backed mortgage securities. To qualify for this category, the majority of a fund's portfolio must always be invested in mortgage-backed securities. ARM funds, for the most part, are short-term GNMA funds whose mortgage interest rates are reset periodically.

Corporate bond funds seek a high level of income by investing the majority of the funds' assets in debt securities issued by corporations. The balance of a portfolio may be invested in U.S. Treasury bonds and bonds of other government entities. Plain vanilla corporate bond funds tend to concentrate their investments in high-quality, investment-grade bonds with agency ratings of A or better.

High-yield bond funds invest in lower quality corporate issues. In recent years, these bonds, which possess a very high degree of risk, have become known as *junk bonds.* After the near collapse of the junk bond market in the late 1980s, a number of junk bond funds upgraded the quality of their holdings. Many of these funds now also invest in investment-grade corporate bonds and, in some instances, government bonds.

As their name implies, *international bond funds* invest in public and private debt of governments and corporations domiciled outside the United States. In addition to credit risks, international bond fund investors face the risk that returns will be impaired by political events or by changing values of international currencies relative to the U.S. dollar.

Advantages of Bond Funds over Bonds

You may ask why you should invest in a bond fund when you can invest directly in bonds themselves. The answer is simple: Bond funds offer several advantages over direct investment in bonds for all but the most well-heeled investors. First, the minimum investment requirements for bond funds are usually far less cumbersome than those for single bonds. Second, by investing in a bond fund, you obtain a significant degree of risk reduction because you own a *pro rata* share of a portfolio containing hundreds of bond issues rather than a small handful of issues. Third, unless you trade millions of dollars of a single bond issue, the transactions costs are relatively high. In fact, the difference between the bid and offer prices for most bonds is so significant that small traders must ante up an entire year's interest income to acquire their bonds. Thus, bond funds boost fixed-income returns by lower trading costs for most individual investors. Finally, as a bond fund investor, you obtain a high degree of liquidity. Because bond funds must redeem shares tendered at the end of a business day, investors with changing investment needs can easily and quickly adjust their bond fund holdings.

Tax-Exempt Bond Funds

Tax-exempt, or municipal, bonds are debt obligations of local and state governments. The interest on these bonds is exempt from federal taxes and from state and local taxes in the states where the bonds are issued. Even though these bonds are said to be tax-exempt, municipal bond investors generally must pay state and local taxes on interest income earned on bonds issued outside an investor's state of residence. In addition, capital gains income earned on municipal bond investments is not exempt from federal or state taxation.

Municipal ("muni") bonds are classified as *general obligation bonds* (interest and principal repayments are met by the taxing power of municipalities and states) or *revenue bonds* (the ability to pay principal and interest is a function of the income earned by facilities such as toll roads, hospitals, etc.). Single-state municipal bond funds are similar to other municipal bond funds except that their portfolios contain the issues of only one state. Residents of that state receive a triple tax advantage because interest income is exempt from federal, state and local taxation.

The Tax Reform Act of 1976 allowed open-end mutual funds to pass through tax-free income to fund shareholders. Prior to the act, only unit investment trusts were granted the tax-free pass-through. As a result, the municipal bond fund emerged when Kemper organized the first open-end municipal bond fund in April 1976. Since then, hundreds of tax-exempt bond funds have come to market.

Not all municipal bond funds are alike. Some invest in only high-quality issues, while others seek a higher current yield by investing in bonds of marginal credit quality (generally revenue bonds). In addition, you can find municipal bond funds whose managers target their average maturities to specific periods, such as short term, intermediate term and long term. Some muni bond funds invest in only insured municipal bonds. The insurance kicks in when a municipality defaults on its debt obligations. If a municipality defaults, the insuring agency makes the bond's scheduled interest payments and will return the principal amount of the bond at its scheduled maturity date, if necessary. Although insured municipal bonds have some appeal, you end up paying the insurance premium by accepting lower interest rates on these bonds.

With the expansion of tax rates levied by states and cities, municipal bonds issued outside an investor's state of residence have lost some of their tax advantage. As a result, a number of mutual fund companies greatly expanded their offerings of single-state municipal bond funds. This has been one of the fastest growing areas in the bond fund category in recent years.

Advantages

Like taxable bonds, municipal bond funds offer shareholders several advantages. First, they offer a high degree of liquidity. Most municipal bonds are traded infrequently; however, municipal bond fund shareholders can purchase or sell their bond fund shares daily. Second, because of the relatively low level of trading activity, municipal bonds possess very wide bid–offer price spreads. Thus, when purchasing or selling municipal bonds directly, investors trading in less than $100,000 lots face trading costs that can easily erase an entire year's interest income. Because muni bond funds purchase large blocks of bonds, they can obtain much more favorable prices than can individual investors. Finally, bond fund investors can obtain significant portfolio diversification with the investment of a modest amount of money, thereby greatly reducing default risk.

Disadvantages

Municipal bonds are not for everyone. Although not being required to ante up tax payments on income offers some appeal, tax avoidance pays off only when the net return from a municipal bond exceeds the after-tax return on a comparable fully taxable bond.

Thus, when comparing municipal bonds with taxable bonds, you must adjust to the tax-exempt yield on a municipal bond to put it on equal footing with a fully taxable bond. Do this by dividing the municipal bond's yield by one minus your marginal tax rate. That gives you the taxable equivalent yield. If this yield exceeds that of a comparable taxable bond's yield, the municipal bond is the better investment.

Example: Suppose that a 20-year municipal bond currently yields 5 percent, while a 20-year fully taxable bond currently yields 7 percent. Suppose further that your marginal tax rate is 28 percent. Divide the muni's 5 percent yield by 1 minus 0.28, or 0.72. That produces a fully taxable yield of 6.94 percent. Because the fully taxable bond possesses a yield greater than the municipal bond's adjusted yield, you would be money ahead by investing in the fully taxable bond rather than the municipal bond.

Money Market Funds

Money market mutual funds, born in the mid-1970s, invest shareholders' capital in debt securities with very short maturities. Some money market funds confine their portfolios to issues of the U.S. government. Others invest in private debt securities, which might include commercial paper (short-term corporate unsecured IOUs), bank certificates of deposit, bankers' acceptances (which arise from international trade transactions) and other short-term debt.

SEC (Securities and Exchange Commission) regulations restrict both the types of securities that money funds can invest in and the composition of their portfolios. Like other mutual funds, a money market fund cannot invest more than 5 percent of its assets in the debt issued by a single company or more than 25 percent of its assets in the debt issues of companies in a single industry. In addition, SEC regulations prohibit a money market fund from investing in commercial paper not included in the two top grades—securities rates A1 and A2 by Standard & Poor's or P1 and P2 by Moody's. Finally, money market funds cannot invest in debt with a maturity of more than 120 days, and the weighted average maturity of their portfolios cannot exceed 90 days.

Money market funds are the least risky of all mutual funds. Those that invest in Treasury bills are nearly free of risk. Some of these funds, however, introduce an element of risk by investing some of their capital in repurchase agreements, or repos. While money market fund investors have never lost one dime of their assets, money funds that invest in private debt subject their shareholders to default risk. In fact, a handful of money market funds suffered losses when several companies defaulted on their commercial paper a few years ago. The advisers of these funds, however, assumed these losses, and money fund shareholders were left untouched when the sponsors reimbursed the funds for the losses incurred.

The popularity of money market funds among savers and investors is understandable. These funds generally pay higher rates of interest than bank savings accounts, they provide shareholders with free checking accounts and they extend wire transfer privileges.

Money market fund share prices are fixed by law at $1. Interest income earned is credited to shareholder accounts daily and is automatically reinvested in additional fund shares. While share prices are fixed, interest rates and therefore interest income can fluctuate daily. Money market funds report their current yields two ways—as annualized seven-day average yields and as annualized seven-day compound yields. At a particular point in time, yields among money funds can vary significantly. These differences arise because of differences in portfolio composition, differences in average maturities and differences in fund expense ratios. Some funds have waived their advisory fees in an attempt to make their yields more attractive to investors. So it's important to look behind the generous yields offered from time to time by some money funds before investing.

In this chapter, I have described the characteristics of the major categories of mutual funds available to individual investors. To determine which funds are right for you, you need solid, reliable data that describe the financial and operating characteristics of individual funds. You can find information in a fund's prospectus and shareholder report. The next chapter describes these documents in great detail.

5

Investigate before You Invest

While you can find an abundance of information on a potential mutual fund investment, you may believe that you do not have the time or the expertise to gather and evaluate such data. While even professional investors lack perfect foresight and thus take investment losses from time to time, they rarely acquire assets that possess risk and return characteristics inconsistent with their investment needs. Before professionals as well as individual investors decide how they expect a fund to perform, they should first evaluate how that investment fits their financial goals and investment philosophies.

When evaluating any investment alternative, start with the question: Is this investment right for me? In the case of mutual fund evaluation, you can find the answer to this question by examining the goals and objectives of the fund, along with fund management's ability to carry out those objectives. Additionally, you must evaluate the services provided by the fund and the costs of such services. You will find this information in the fund's prospectus. While the law mandates that each fund must send a prospectus to all potential investors before it can accept your application, I have found that many mutual fund investors do not read this important document before investing. These individuals are generally surprised when they incur unexpected charges for services provided, when they don't obtain the services they thought the fund provided or when the value of their fund shares fluctuates abnormally. Following are just a few examples of what can happen to those who don't take the time to read a fund's prospectus before investing.

Many investors in the 44 Wall Street Fund were shocked when their fund shares took a nosedive even though the stock market as a whole underwent only a moderate correction. Many of these individuals were surprised to learn that fund management used leverage in managing the portfolio. Furthermore, they were shocked to find that the fund was characterized as nondiversified because it held fewer than a dozen stocks in its portfolio at the time of the price plunge. This information, of course, was spelled out in the fund's prospectus. Many had ignored that document in their rush to invest in a fund that had climbed to the top of the performance ladder.

I have seen investors quarrel with fund management when they were charged unexpected fees on premature redemptions. Others have been dismayed to learn that they could not switch their investment from one fund in the family to another until a 30-day waiting period had elapsed. Still others were dumbfounded when they received a large distribution (fully taxable) shortly after they had made a purchase. These investors all had one thing in common: They had not read the fund's prospectus.

How Your Money Will Be Invested

Before investing in any fund, request and read the following documents: the prospectus and the statement of additional information, the annual shareholders' report and the latest quarterly or semiannual report. Here's what to look for.

Reading the Prospectus

The fund's prospectus contains several sections that spell out what management will do with your money.

Investment objectives and policies In this section, the fund spells out its investment objectives and the strategies that it will use to pursue these goals. Some funds merely tell you that they will invest your money in stocks and bonds and that they will emphasize current income, capital growth or both.

SMART STRATEGIES *Before investing in any fund, request and read the prospectus, statement of additional information, annual shareholders' report and latest quarterly or semiannual report.*

Others quite specifically spell out their investment philosophies. My advice to you is consider only those funds that are quite specific about their investment goals, philosophies and portfolio management strategies.

Risk factors A fundamental axiom of investing is that investment risk always accompanies investment return. The greater the anticipated rewards from an investment, the greater the risks you assume as an investor. While this is a basic tenet of the investment world, some investors who seek the largest returns possible often forget that such assets can be very risky. These individuals frequently select mutual funds solely on the basis of recent performance. Because many of these investors don't examine how the funds earned such short-term returns, they are often perplexed when the high performance falters.

Fund expenses Make no initial investment in any mutual fund until you determine what it will cost to make that investment. (Chapter 7 outlines the costs of mutual fund investing.) Sales charges and fund operating expenses can erode investment returns significantly. By law, the mutual fund prospectus must estimate all costs associated with an investment in the fund, including sales charges and operating expenses. (See Figure 5.1.) These expenses are expressed as percentages of the fund's NAV and are displayed prominently near the beginning of the prospectus. In addition, the

FIGURE 5.1 □ Sample Mutual Fund Expense Report

The following information is provided to assist you in understanding the various costs and expenses that a shareholder of the Fund will bear directly or indirectly. There are certain charges associated with retirement accounts and with certain services offered by the Fund. See "SHAREHOLDER PLANS." Purchases and redemptions also may be made through broker-dealers or others who may charge a commission or other transaction fee for their services. The Annual Fund Operating Expenses are actual expenses incurred during the fiscal year ended October 31, 1992. The adviser will waive its management fee (0.7%) to the extent that the Fund's total operating expenses exceed 2.5% of the average net assets. See "MANAGEMENT OF THE FUND." The example below is based on the Annual Fund Operating Expenses set forth in the accompanying table.

Shareholder Transaction Expenses

Maximum Sales Load Imposed on Purchases or Reinvested Dividends	None
Deferred Sales Load	None
Redemption Fee	None
Exchange Fee	None

Annual Fund Operating Expenses

Management Fee	0.7%
12b-1 Fees	None
Other Expenses	1.6%
Total Fund Operating Expenses	2.3%

Example:	1 Year	3 Years	5 Years	10 Years
You would pay the following expenses on a $1,000 investment, assuming (1) 5% annual return and (2) redemption at the end of each time period:	$23	$71	$121	$259

The example should not be considered a representation of past or future expenses and actual expenses may be greater or less than these shown.

prospectus must illustrate the total dollar cost you might pay if you invest in the fund for one, three or five years.

Investment restrictions The Investment Company Act of 1940 limits mutual funds in their investments, and these investment restrictions are repeated in this section. Figure 5.2 provides an example of investment restrictions. However, because many funds place additional restrictions on their investment advisors' activities, you should read this section carefully.

FIGURE 5.2 □ Investment Restrictions

1. The Fund will not purchase securities on margin, participate in a joint trading account, sell securities short, or act as an underwriter or distributor of securities other than its own capital stock.
2. The Fund will not purchase or sell real estate or interests in real estate, commodities or commodity futures. The Fund may invest in the securities of real estate investment trusts, but not more than 10% in value of the Fund's total assets will be so invested. Less than 5% of the Fund's total net assets were at risk in the securities of real estate investment trusts in the past year. The Fund does not currently intend to place at risk more than 5% of its total net assets in such investments in the foreseeable future.
3. The Fund may make temporary bank borrowings (not in excess of 5% of the lower of cost or market value of the Fund's total assets) for emergency or extraordinary purposes.
4. Not more than 5% of the total assets of the Fund, taken at market value, will be invested in the securities of any one issuer (not including United States Government securities).
5. Not more than 25% of the Fund's total assets will be concentrated in companies of any one industry or group of related industries.

Prospectus Parts A and B

A few years ago, the SEC found that, because prospectuses were written in "legalese," prospective fund investors frequently did not read them. As a result, the SEC allowed mutual funds to split their prospectuses into two parts. Many funds have opted to relegate the legal descriptions of their intended operations to Part B of the prospectus, called the Statement of Additional Information. (See Figure 5.3.) This document is available to prospective investors free of charge on request. Although admittedly these documents make boring reading, they represent elements of the contract between you and the fund. Therefore, I recommend that prospective investors take a few minutes to examine this document.

Shareholders' Reports

Once you have perused a fund's prospectus and its Statement of Additional Information, turn your attention to its annual (or semi-annual) shareholders' report. Recently, the SEC revised the reporting requirements for this document, which has made it much more informative. First, examine the portfolio manager's discussion of the fund's recent performance. (See Figure 5.4.)

Net asset value (for no-load funds) is synonymous with share price. Investment income consists of all dividend and interest payments a fund receives plus realized short-term capital gains on its investments. *Dividends* from net investment income are payments made to shareholders. The ratio of net investment income to average net assets is actually the *average current yield* a fund earns.

Portfolio turnover rate measures a mutual fund's purchase and sales activity. You calculate it by dividing the lesser of purchases or sales for the fiscal year by the monthly average value of the securities owned by the fund during that year. However, securities with maturities of less than one year are excluded from the calculation. A portfolio turnover of 100 percent indicates a complete turnover of fund assets. The fund's adviser is now required to indicate whether the fund performed as it has in the recent past. The discussion must include any special circumstances that may have positively or negatively affected its recent returns. In addition, the report must contain a graph of a hypothetical $10,000 investment

FIGURE 5.3 □ Condensed Financial Information

FINANCIAL HIGHLIGHTS	Years Ended October 31				
	1993	**1992**	**1991**	**1990**	**1989**
Selected Per-Share Data					
Net asset value, beginning of a period	11.43	$11.36	$8.17	$10.52	$10.22
Income from investment operations					
Net investment income (loss)	(0.14)	(0.12)	(0.02)	0.09	0.16
Net realized and unrealized gain (loss) on investments	1.61	0.31	3.27	(2.27)	0.22
Total from investment operations	1.47	0.19	3.25	(2.18)	0.38
Less distributions:					
From net investment income	(0.08)	—	(0.06)	(0.17)	(0.08)
From net realized gain	(0.28)	(0.12)	—	—	—
Total distributions	(0.36)	(0.12)	(0.06)	(0.17)	(0.08)
Net asset value, end of period	$12.54	$11.43	$11.36	$8.17	$10.52
Total Return	12.97%	1.70%	40.06%	(21.07)%	3.75%
Ratios and Supplemental Data					
Net assets, end of period (in thousands)	$7,208	$6,942	$6,183	$4,265	$5,573
Ratio of expenses to average net assets	1.96%	2.31%	2.50%	2.50%	2.50%
Ratio of net investment income to average net assets	(1.1%)	(1.1%)	(0.2%)	0.9%	1.8%
Portfolio turnover rate	34.6%	24.4%	37.4%	23.6%	22.6%

The accompanying notes to financial statements are an integral part of this statement.

FIGURE 5.4 □ Sample Required Fund Performance in Shareholder's Report

You have several ways to evaluate a fund's historical performance. You can look at the total percentage change in value, the average annual percentage change or the growth of a hypothetical $10,000 investment. Each performance figure includes changes in the fund's share price, plus reinvestment of any dividends (or income) and capital gains (the profits the fund earns when it sells stocks that have grown in value)

	Cumulative Total Returns	
Periods ended September 30, 1993	Past 1 Year	Life of Fund
ABC Fund	19.71%	95.40%
S&P 500®	13.00	93.47
Average Flexible Portfolio Fund	14.10	74.25
Consumer Price Index	2.69	20.41

Cumulative total returns reflect the fund's actual performance over a set period—in this case, one year or since the fund began on December 28, 1988. For example, if you invested $1,000 in a fund that had a 5 percent return over one year, you would end up with $1,050. You can compare the fund's returns to those of the S&P 500—a common proxy for the U.S. stock market. You also can compare them to the average flexible portfolio fund, which currently reflects the performance of 68 funds tracked by Lipper Analytical Services. Both benchmarks include reinvested dividends and capital gains, if any, and exclude the effect of sales charges. Comparing the fund's performance to the Consumer Price Index helps show how your investment compared to inflation.

	Average Annual Total Returns	
Periods ended September 30, 1993	Past 1 Year	Life of Fund
ABC Fund	19.71%	15.10%
S&P 500®	13.00	14.86
Average Flexible Portfolio Fund	14.10	12.30
Consumer Price Index	2.69	3.99

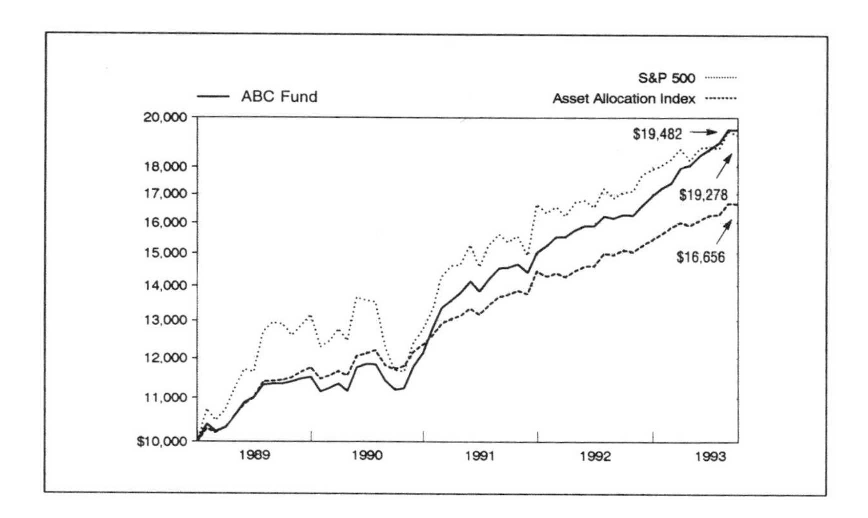

in the fund, along with a graph of the performance of an "appropriate" market index that reflects the type of investments in the fund's portfolio. Finally, the annual or semiannual report must contain a table listing the fund's average annual total returns for the past year, the past five years and the life of the fund. It must also compare these returns to those of an appropriate market index and the percentage changes in the Consumer Price Index.

It is also important to check the tenure of the fund's portfolio manager. If you base your decision to invest in the fund on its past performance, you want to know whether the current portfolio manager is responsible for that performance. By law, the fund must present a biography of its portfolio manager in either the fund's annual report or its prospectus.

Briefly review the fund's financial highlights presented in the shareholders' report. This summary contains financial statistics for the lesser of each of the last ten years or the life of the fund. Important statistics include the ratio of expenses to average net assets, the ratio of net investment income to average net assets, and the fund's annual portfolio turnover rate.

Finally, review the fund's investments contained in the statement of net assets. Are these the types of investments you expected to find in the fund? Could particular types of assets cause problems (e.g., private placements, restricted securities or financial derivatives)? Is the fund well diversified, or does it concentrate its investments in a few assets or select industries? Obtaining the answers to these questions before you invest in the fund can save you a lot of grief later.

If you planned to hand over your money to a professional asset manager, you would most likely interview that manager before signing an investment management contract. You would probably want to know what the services would cost, how your money would be invested, what returns you could expect and what risks would be taken in pursuing your investment objectives. Take the same care when investing in a mutual fund. Although most likely you will not be able to interview the fund's portfolio manager, the fund's prospectus and shareholders' reports contain the answers to the questions you should ask before you make an initial investment in the fund. It pays to investigate before you invest.

6

Investing in the Best Mutual Funds

Begin the process of weeding out unacceptable funds by examining a few "housekeeping" tips.

1. *Find out whether the fund is registered for sale in your state of residence.* Generally, if it is not registered in your state, the fund will not send a prospectus. However, slip-ups can occur.
2. *Check the list of services the fund provides.* Are they the services you desire (e.g., wire transfers, telephone ex-changes, IRAs, Keoghs, etc.)?
3. *Determine whether the fund is scheduled to pay a distribution in the near future.* As we saw in Chapter 3, you won't necessarily reject a fund if it has scheduled one, but you may save a few tax dollars if you postpone buying initial shares until after the distribution has been paid.
4. *Consider all purchase and redemption fees, and determine whether the fees are excessive.* For example, when making an IRA or a Keogh purchase, consider all sales charges excessive because they are taken off the front end. The result is that the actual investment amount will be less than

the maximum allowable retirement plan contribution for a given year.

After you have weeded out funds based on these tips, use the following guidelines to help you narrow your search for the funds best suited for you.

General Guidelines To Help You Choose Your Mutual Funds

I recommend that you select only those mutual funds registered with the SEC (Securities and Exchange Commission). Avoid so-called "offshore" or foreign-based mutual funds. While many of these unregistered funds may provide ways to hide investment dollars and income from Uncle Sam's tax department, the funds do not offer the federal government's protection against malpractice or fraud. Remember, there is no such thing as a free lunch. Increased investment risks (including the risk that someone will steal your money) accompany the additional return offshore mutual funds promise.

I also recommend that you invest in only mutual funds whose NAVs (net asset values) are reported in *The Wall Street Journal* or *Barron's* magazine. All funds with at least 1,000 shareholders report their daily NAVs to the automatic quotation services provided by the National Association of Securities Dealers (NASD) and, in turn, the NAVs are reported to the financial press. Because of the proliferation of funds in recent years, some general circulation newspapers have limited the number of funds they report on. Many now report daily prices for only those funds with more than $30 million in total assets. However, financial publications such as *The Wall Street Journal, Investors' Business Daily* and *Barron's* report the prices of all funds listed on Nasdaq (NASD's Automated Quotation system). By following this rule, you may miss the opportunity to invest in tiny funds that may possess great performance potential. However, the small size of such funds may hinder their performance. Furthermore, to track your overall performance over time, it is essential that you be able to obtain accurate and up-to-date share-price data.

I also suggest that you avoid newly offered funds. Unlike "hot" new stock issues, offered at prices set deliberately low to generate investor interest, mutual fund shares are offered at NAV (plus a sales charge, if it is a load fund). Thus, you have little advantage in getting in on the ground floor. Furthermore, when you evaluate a fund, determine how fund management copes with changing market conditions. A little operating history is required. We recommend that you make no purchase until fund shares have been offered to the general public for at least one year. Note, we did not say "one-year-old." Many new funds are started as limited partnerships. If a fund has a good track record, it is taken public. Thus, for many new funds, the great returns advertised in the press were available to only a few investors. The so-called *embryo* funds that do not perform well initially are never taken public. Be wary of new funds with great track records that started out as embryo funds.

In addition, avoid those mutual funds that can or do invest in letter-stock or other unregistered securities. Because these assets are infrequently traded, current value is difficult to assess. Management can easily inflate (or deflate) NAV by making subjective valuations of these assets. Furthermore, because the assets are not liquid, a fund may not be able to dispose of them when market conditions or corporate fortunes change.

One of the most important guidelines I can offer is to assess whether a fund's objective is appropriate for you. Does it correspond with your overall portfolio risk and return plan, given your investment philosophy? The stated objective of the fund you are considering should be specific, understandable and consistent with your needs and desires.

While law requires that every prospectus contain a description of the fund's investment objectives, clarity is not mandated. The objectives contained in some mutual fund prospectuses are so garbled and nebulous that it is difficult to tell what management will do with your money. I suggest that, if the objective is unclear, you pass over that fund and look for another.

If, after examining the fund's investment objectives, you appear to have found a match between your personal objectives and the fund's investment objectives, your next step is to examine the fund's financial record, which we discussed in Chapter 5. This segment of the prospectus contains a summary of the audited annual reports of the fund for the past ten years (if the fund is that old). You can use the data provided in the statement of condensed financial information to apply several additional screens. First, examine the fund's total assets. I recommend that you eliminate aggressive growth common stock funds with total assets greater than $400 million from your list. Do retain growth (or growth and income) funds with assets up to $1 billion. For bond funds, the greater the level of total assets, the better, because bond funds with sizable assets tend to possess wider diversification and lower expense ratios.

While there exists little scientific documentation of the impact of asset size on mutual fund performance, investment theory suggests that smaller funds may be better able to outperform the market averages than giant funds. For example, a $2 billion fund that holds 400 or 500 different stocks has literally "bought the market." As a result, its returns will, for the most part, parallel those of the market averages. Secondly, such funds generally possess large holdings of individual stocks; thus, their disposal could unfavorably affect share price and dampen the funds' returns. Thirdly, some portfolio managers have candidly conceded that management of a fund becomes difficult when assets exceed $400 million to $500 million. Operational inefficiencies and increased expenses may begin to appear when a fund's assets (and the number of shareholders) pass some total asset threshold. Finally, because optimal portfolio diversification can be obtained with as few as 40 to 50 different common stock issues, larger funds generally provide superfluous diversification.

As we saw in Chapter 5, portfolio turnover is the lesser of purchases or sales for the fiscal year divided by average net assets. This reflects how frequently a fund buys and sells securities. You can use the following equation to translate the turnover rate into the average holding period of the portfolio: 1 divided by the turnover rate (expressed as a decimal). For example, a fund with a 50 percent turnover rate has an average holding period of two years, calculated as follows:

$$\frac{1}{0.50} = 2 \text{ years}$$

Avoid mutual funds with historical portfolio turnover rates greater than 100 percent. These funds, on average, possess securities holding periods of less than one year. Thus, it is quite possible that, in periods of sustained increases in stock prices, such a fund may have been caught at year-end with substantial net realized capital gains. Because funds with low portfolio turnover ratios possess long-term average holding periods (a 25 percent turnover implies an average four-year holding period), the realized gains distributed to shareholders will most likely be minimal.

In addition, avoid funds with high portfolio turnover rates because a high turnover rate means greater brokerage costs for a fund. The relatively high transaction costs mutual funds incur could cause the net investment return of high-portfolio-turnover funds to be much smaller than would be the case if portfolio turnover were lower. Brokerage costs are directly reflected in the price of the securities a fund buys. I also recommend that you seek mutual funds with some degree of concentration of assets. (Remember, funds that possess widely distributed assets may have bought the market and thus be relegated to returns paralleling market rates of return.) This screen already may have been satisfied when you applied the size screen. However, you can assess the degree of assets concentration directly by examining the number of common stocks held. I prefer funds with fewer than 200 stocks. You only can obtain your goal of earning a rate of return greater than the market rate of return from portfolios that do not mirror the market.

You also may obtain a degree of asset concentration by investing in funds that specialize in stocks of a particular industry (technology, utilities, etc.) or those funds that invest in special situations (out-of-favor companies, low-price-earnings stocks, small equity capitalization firms, etc.). Remember, however, along with increased concentration comes increased investment risk. Remember, also, you can't beat the market if you own it. This warrants some degree of asset concentration.

I also suggest taking a cursory glance at a fund's average expense ratio and management fee schedule. Give preference to funds with expense ratios that average less than 1.5 percent and to management fees that average less than 0.75 percent of average annual assets. Remember, the higher the expenses, the lower the return to shareholders (all other things being equal).

Finally, obtain as much information as you can regarding fund management. Because the manager makes portfolio purchase and sales decisions, the quality of management frequently determines performance. I like funds to possess a continuity of management. If portfolio managers have been investing for a long time, they have gained experience in trading in various types of markets. In addition, they know how they will react to a rapid change in market conditions. I also prefer to invest in mutual funds whose management possesses a well-defined investment philosophy and can articulate its strategies for trading in various types of markets.

Although collecting financial and operating statistics for many mutual funds may be a formidable task, a number of mutual fund advisory services now make these statistics available on a regular basis at a modest cost. (See the Appendix for a description of the major mutual fund statistical and advisory services.)

Making Your Final Selections

I recommend that growth-oriented investors seek growth and aggressive growth funds with betas greater than 1.00. *Beta* measures the relative systematic risk of an asset or a portfolio. It relates the volatility of the asset compared to the market as a whole (usually the S&P 500 stock index). I prefer investment in high-beta funds because even though stock prices rise and fall over short-term periods, over the longer term, stock prices have always moved to a higher level. Thus, long-term-oriented investors will find that higher beta portfolios will rise in value by more than the percentage long-term rise in stock market prices. For example, the Twentieth Century equity funds possess betas greater than 1.25. Although highly volatile, these funds have delivered exceptional returns over periods of 5, 10 and 15 years.

Although some financial writers claim that examining a fund's portfolio of assets provides little guidance in fund selection, I strongly disagree. I believe that analyzing a growth fund's or an aggressive growth fund's individual stocks is tantamount to fund selection. Before I present a method for analysis, let's look at the reasons others believe that fund stock analysis is frivolous. First, some argue that the common stock holdings of mutual funds listed in their quarterly (or annual) financial reports do not represent of current stock holdings. However, I have suggested that fund investors select mutual funds that possess low portfolio turnover ratios; therefore, it is highly likely that the stocks listed in their financial reports will represent the funds' current asset holdings. Secondly, some financial writers believe that nonprofessional investors lack the expertise and skill to analyze individual common stocks. This, I believe, insults the average investor. Finally, some believe that the common stock holdings of most mutual funds are too extensive to allow timely and meaningful analysis. To some extent, that is true. However, if you focus on a fund's 20 or 30 largest investments, I believe you will get the flavor of the fund's investment style.

Focus your attention on five variables: (1) price-earnings (PE) ratio, (2) growth rate, (3) dividend yield, (4) ratio of current stock price to book value per share and (5) average equity capitalization. Both *Morningstar Mutual Funds* and *The Value Line Mutual Fund Survey* list these statistics for the equity funds they cover.

The objective of this exercise is not to second-guess fund management, but to find out what a fund's portfolio actually contains. Many individuals, especially those influenced by near-term past performance figures, invest in a fund without knowing what kinds of stock the fund holds. For example, if you find that a fund holds shares of stock with average PE multiples of 30 times recent earnings, average dividend yields of 0.20 percent and average annual growth rates of 30 percent, you have found a very aggressive fund. That fact is neither good nor bad. However, if you have a very conservative investment philosophy, an investment in such a fund, regardless of past performance, may not be *your* best choice. Similarly, if you plan to invest in a small-cap fund, avoid those funds that have invested in stocks with equity capitalizations exceeding $300 million. In short, before investing in any equity fund, look before you leap.

Up to this point, I have carefully avoided the issue of using historical mutual fund returns as a basis for selecting funds with superior future performance potential (or avoiding those with inferior performance potential). Several academic researchers have tested the ability of mutual fund managers to consistently outperform the market. In one study of 39 common stock funds, Eugene Fama found none that consistently earned net returns great enough to place it among the top 20 funds in each of the ten years studied. In another study, William Sharpe found that, on average, the returns from 34 mutual funds fell short of the returns that could have been obtained by an investor following a naive buy-and-hold strategy (random selection and wide diversification). A study by Professor M. C. Jensen showed that 115 mutual funds, on average, were not able to forecast future securities prices well enough to recover their research expenses, management fees and commission costs.

The evidence provided by these studies (along with several others) strongly suggests that looking at how a fund has performed does not tell you how well it will do. A fund that beats the market during a previous period has about a 50-50 chance of beating the market in a future period. The odds are the same for a fund that did not beat the market in a previous period. These odds imply that, on the basis of historical return alone, you could do just as well at selecting superior-performing funds with a coin flip. However, if you feel more confident basing your final choice on historical data (after screening funds on the criteria outlined earlier), I see no adverse consequences.

In fact, if the increase in your confidence leads to longer holding periods than otherwise would be the case, there may be some implicit benefit in selecting only top-rated funds. This is because, time and again, it has been demonstrated that investors with longer holding periods generally obtain larger investment returns than those with shorter holding periods. Transaction costs, research costs and tax effects more than cancel any advantage that the short-term trader may possess.

SMART STRATEGIES *You can generally obtain larger investment returns if you hold onto your funds for longer time spans than if you hold them for shorter ones.*

Does this mean that historical data give little guidance in making fund selection? No. Funds that have performed well, *relative to the performance of their peers,* are more desirable investments than are those funds whose returns continuously fall short of those of their peers. Thus, once you have found a handful of funds with an investment style that meets your investment needs, objectives and risk tolerance level, compare its returns to those of its peers over periods of one, three and five years. Invest in those funds that consistently rank above average in performance. Chances are these funds will continue to deliver above-average performance, given their investment style and level of risk.

Has the Fund Conformed to Its Stated Policies and Objectives?

Although many fund investors spend the bulk of their time looking for funds that will perform the best, less than 20 percent of the return you will eventually earn on your mutual fund portfolio will result from fund selection. Instead, long-term investment performance is dominated by asset allocation decisions: the categories of assets you hold and the percentage allocation you make to each category.

So before you begin to look for individual funds, concentrate on asset allocation decisions. That means you must know who you are and what you want your mutual fund portfolio to do for you. The fund selection process begins with a list of the categories of assets you wish to include in your portfolio (e.g., aggressive growth funds, international equity funds, sector funds, etc.). Once you have made this list, establish the percentage of your portfolio that you plan to allocate to each category. Next, examine the risk and return characteristics of this portfolio. If your initial allocations will not provide the return you desire or if the intended portfolio contains more risk than you can tolerate, adjust the target allocations until you match your objectives with the portfolio's financial characteristics. Only then should you embark on a search for "the best" mutual funds.

7

The Mutual Fund Game: What Does It Cost To Play?

When investing in mutual funds, or any asset for that matter, you should first consider the costs of obtaining, maintaining and eventually liquidating the investment. Transactions and portfolio maintenance costs reduce investment returns and, thus, you should consider and weigh them against potential returns when making any investment. Again, for mutual funds, the prospectus contains the data needed to evaluate cost.

The costs you incur as a mutual fund investor fall into three categories: sales commissions, management fees and general operating expenses. Until recently, you needed to do some digging to uncover all of these various fees and expenses. However, the SEC has handed down regulations that simplify this process by requiring mutual funds to list these items prominently in a table located within the first few pages of the prospectus. While this fee table does not relieve you of your responsibility to read the entire prospectus, it should help reduce the time you spend playing detective.

Also, contained in the "Investment Adviser" section of the prospectus is a description of the contract between the fund and the investment adviser. The compensation paid to the adviser is described here, along with a listing of those operating expenses the adviser incurs and those fund shareholders assume.

The *expense ratio* is the total of management fees and general operating expenses paid by shareholders divided by average total assets under management. The average expense ratio for common stock funds is around 1.5 percent, for bond funds, the average expense ratio is around 0.8 percent.

Most investors won't buy a new suit or a pair of shoes without first knowing the price. In fact, most individuals shop around and pride themselves on obtaining the best available prices for many of the things they buy. However, when investing in mutual funds, many people pay no attention to the cost of investing. In fact, I have met few mutual fund investors who know what they pay to invest in mutual funds. To these individuals, I say: First find out what you will pay; then shop around to get the best price available.

The Costs of Mutual Fund Investing

Sales charges Mutual funds come in two varieties–those with sales charges and those without. Funds with sales charges are *front-end load funds,* which take sales fees right off the top. For example, if you invest $1,000 in an 8.5 percent front-end load fund, you pay $85 in commission, and the balance, $915, is invested in fund shares. (Note that an 8.5 percent front-end load turns out to be 9.3 percent of the money actually invested in the fund.) These days, very few funds charge the maximum load allowable under the law (8.5 percent). Of the funds sold with front-end loads, most add sales charges that range from 3 percent to 5 percent of the amount of money invested.

Some funds have opted to forgo the front-end sales charge and take their fees off the back end, instead. These are called *contingent deferred sales charge funds* because the back-end commission is reduced in relation to the length of time you retain your shares. For example, many of these funds levy a 5 percent charge if you withdraw an investment within one year. The fee is reduced by one percentage point for each additional year you hold the fund shares. Thus, the sales charge completely disappears if you keep the investment five or more years.

Other mutual funds levy ongoing sales charges rather than either front-end or back-end loads. These charges, called *12b-1 fees,* typically average about 0.50 percent annually, but can range from 0.10 percent to 0.75 percent of the value of your investment. Note that while these percentages appear lower than those applied to either front-end or back-end load funds, they are levied each year instead of only once.

Finally, some funds combine 12b-1 charges with back-end loads. (In fact, most back-end load funds come with 12b-1 charges attached.) Note that the longer you hold the shares of such funds, the lower the contingent deferred sales charges, but the greater the total 12b-1 fees. Thus, for these funds, what you gain on the one hand you often lose on the other.

Management and administrative fees While some individuals pay a sales charge when they invest in mutual funds (those who invest in load funds) and some do not (those who invest in no-load funds), all mutual fund investors must pay annual fund management and administrative fees. Management fees are paid to the fund's investment adviser and generally range from 0.50 percent to 1.0 percent of the fund's average assets. Typically, the management fee percentage decreases as the fund's total assets increase.

In addition to management fees, fund shareholders must foot the bill for such administrative items as shareholder recordkeeping, auditing, legal services, shareholders' reports, the annual meeting, custodial fees and so on. Management and administrative fees for a typical equity fund range from 0.20 percent to 2.5 percent and average about 1.5 percent of the fund's total assets. (The combined management and administrative expenses for the typical bond fund average about 0.80 percent of total assets.)

Transactions costs Finally, mutual fund investors assume the transactions costs that occur when a portfolio manager adds securities to the fund's portfolio or deletes them. Transactions costs include both brokerage commissions and the dealer's bid-ask spread. These charges average about 2 percent of the value of each transaction, or about 4 percent to both buy and sell the same stock. These expenses, of course, relate to the fund's portfolio turnover rate. For example, if a portfolio manager were to sell all of the fund's holdings and replace them with other securities once each year, portfolio turnover would equal 100 percent.

Remember that the reciprocal of the turnover ratio provides a reasonable estimate of a fund's average holding period. For example, a turnover ratio of 50 percent implies that the fund holds its investments an average of two years, while a 25 percent turnover ratio indicates a four-year average holding period.

How You Can Estimate the Cost

The best way to estimate the cost of investing in a particular mutual fund is by examining historical costs. You can find these in the fund's prospectus, statement of additional information and most recent annual report. (Examine all three documents before making any fund investment.)

First, look at the fund's summary of per-share income and capital changes presented in its prospectus. There you will find the fund's historical ratio of expenses to average net assets. This ratio equals management fees and administrative expenses divided by average net assets. Because this ratio tends to decline as a fund's assets grow, sometimes you must forecast asset size to obtain a reliable estimate of next year's ratio. For example, suppose a fund charges a management fee of 0.75 percent and incurred administrative expenses of $250,000 last year. Its average net assets the past year were $50 million, and its expense ratio was 1.25 percent. However, suppose the fund ended the year with $100 million in total assets, and you expect this figure to increase to $150 million by year-end. Thus, you expect net assets for the fund to average $125 million and expenses to total about $1.24 million (a $300,000 estimate of administrative fees plus $937,500 in management fees). An estimate of the total expense ratio for the year turns out to be 1 percent ($1.24 million divided by $125 million).

Transactions charges are the most difficult to assess. While mutual funds report their brokerage expenses, these expenses are only a small portion of transactions costs. The bid-ask spread paid to the market maker is the largest component. The fund does not report this figure in its prospectus or annual shareholders' report; therefore, you must estimate it. Because both brokerage commissions and the dealer's bid-ask spread average about 4 percent on a round-trip trade, you can estimate total transactions costs by multiplying the fund's average turnover ratio by 4 percent.

Use the average of the fund's turnover ratios for the past three years. For example, suppose a fund's portfolio turnover ratios for the last three years were 25, 17 and 21 percent. The average ratio is 21 percent. Multiplying this ratio by 4 percent gives a 0.80 percent estimate of transactions costs. Of course, actual transactions costs depend on *next* year's portfolio turnover ratio. However, because these ratios tend to be stable over time for many funds, a three-year average of historical turnover ratios generally provides an accurate estimate of next year's ratio.

Assessing the Total Cost of Fund Investing

Before you begin analyzing the cost of mutual fund investment, determine how long you plan to hold the fund. Because mutual funds levy some costs only once while they assess other charges each year, the total cost of investing will vary according to your holding period.

Figure 7.1 is a simplified case study of fund expense analysis. It assumes that you plan to invest in a fund and hold it for three years. You have narrowed the alternatives to four funds, and you will choose the fund with the lowest cost.

Fund A has a deferred contingent sales charge that begins at 5 percent, but will be trimmed to 3 percent if you hold the shares for three years. In addition, the fund levies an annual 12b-1 fee of 0.50 percent. The management fee is 0.75 percent annually, and you estimate that administrative fees will amount to 0.30 percent each year. The fund turns over about 25 percent of its portfolio annually ($.25 \times .04 = .01$; $.01 \times 3 = .03$, or 3 percent transactions costs).

Fund B carries an 8.5 percent front-end load, but no 12b-1 or back-end sales fees. Management fees are 1 percent per year, and you estimate that administrative fees will be an additional 0.40 percent annually. The fund turns over about 50 percent of its portfolio each year.

Fund C is a low-load fund, with a 3 percent front-end load, but no 12b-1 or back-end fees. The annual management fee is 0.75 per-

FIGURE 7.1 □ Determining the Cost of Mutual Funds

	Fund A	Fund B	Fund C	Fund D
Sales Charges				
Front-end	0.00%	8.50%	3.00%	0.00%
Back-end	3.00	0.00	0.00	0.00
12b-1	1.50	0.00	0.00	0.00
Expense Ratio				
Management Fee	2.25	3.00	2.25	2.10
Admin. Expenses	0.90	1.20	0.60	0.90
Transactions Costs	3.00	6.00	12.00	2.40
Total Costs	10.65%	18.70%	17.85%	5.40%
Average Annual Cost*	3.55%	6.23%	5.95%	1.80%

*The estimated holding period is three years.

cent, and administrative fees should average 0.20 percent each year. This fund is actively managed, and portfolio turnover has averaged 100 percent per year.

Fund D is a true no-load fund and has no sales charges of any kind. The annual management fee for the fund is 0.70 percent, and administrative expenses are estimated at 0.30 percent annually. Portfolio turnover is low, averaging 20 percent each year.

Figure 7.1 illustrates the total estimated costs for the intended three-year holding period and the average annual cost for each fund. Although the analysis does not make adjustments for the time value of money and thus may not be precise, (for example, a 3 percent back-end fee paid three years from now has a present worth of approximately 2.3 percent when discounted at 10 percent), an unadjusted analysis is sufficient.

Note that 12b-1 fees, management fees and administrative expenses have been multiplied by 3—the intended holding period. Note also that total and average annual costs can vary substantially. Finally, note that, for some funds, the average annual cost can erode return significantly. For example, the management of Fund B must overcome a hefty burden of 6.23 percent annually or 4.43 percent more than Fund D to produce the same investor return.

While some funds are better managed than others and thus provide greater investment returns to their shareholders, over an investment lifetime, frequently the cost of investing makes the difference between investment success and investment failure.

SMART STRATEGIES *The easiest way to increase your investment return is to reduce the cost of investing. Do not make an investment in* any *fund until you have documented all costs and have compared them with similar funds.*

8

Don't Forget about Risk

Many individual investors define investment success as "beating the market," or, in other words, earning above-average returns. But many investors often forget that pursuing greater-than-average returns generally means assuming greater-than-average risk. Because investment risk is defined as variability of investment return, portfolios with above-average return potential are subject to above-average swings in value relative to the stock market as a whole. These portfolios far outpace the market when the market rises but drop faster than the market when the market falls.

However, when stock prices rise, investors tend to forget about the negative aspects of holding a high-risk portfolio because they are beating the market. In fact, I have found that as long as stock prices continue to rise, investors often increase the risk of their portfolios in pursuit of greater and greater investment rewards. These investors are generally shaken by the size of their losses when the stock market takes a sudden dip.

You must continually monitor the riskiness of your investment portfolios. Periodically ask yourself whether the current level of portfolio risk is consistent with your ability to weather sudden investment storms. Although you will be happy when the markets are up, you must decide whether you can live with the loss in wealth that will surely take place during down markets.

How Risky Are Your Mutual Funds?

For diversified portfolios, such as common stock mutual funds, beta provides a useful index of investment risk. Simply stated, *beta* measures portfolio risk in relation to the riskiness of the S&P 500 stock index (i.e., the market).

Figure 8.1 illustrates the trade-off between investment risk and investment return with what is known as the *capital market line.* This upward sloping line represents the combinations of risk and return found in well-diversified portfolios. You can calculate the return potential of a diversified common stock portfolio by applying the following mathematical statement of the capital market line:

$$\text{Portfolio Return} = \text{Risk-Free Return} + \beta \left(\text{Market Return} - \text{Risk-Free Return} \right)$$

The *risk-free rate of return* (RF) is approximately the same as the yield on short-term Treasury bills, while the *market return* (RM) is usually considered the total rate of return on the S&P 500 stock index. For example, if you expect the market to return 12 percent during the next 12 months, and the RF is 6 percent, you can expect a portfolio whose beta is 0.50 to return 9 percent.

$$\text{Portfolio Return} = .06 + 0.5\,(.12 - .06) = .09, \text{ or } 9\%$$

You could expect a portfolio with a beta of 1.5 to return 15 percent. If the market were to fall by 12 percent, the lower beta portfolio would be expected to *decline* by 9 percent, and the high beta portfolio would be expected to decline by 15 percent.

Although beta cannot predict the direction the stock market will take, it anticipates the responsiveness of a portfolio's value extremely well, given changes in the stock market as a whole. For example, if the stock market declined by 50 percent over a pro-

FIGURE 8.1 □ Portfolio Risk and Return: The Capital Market Line

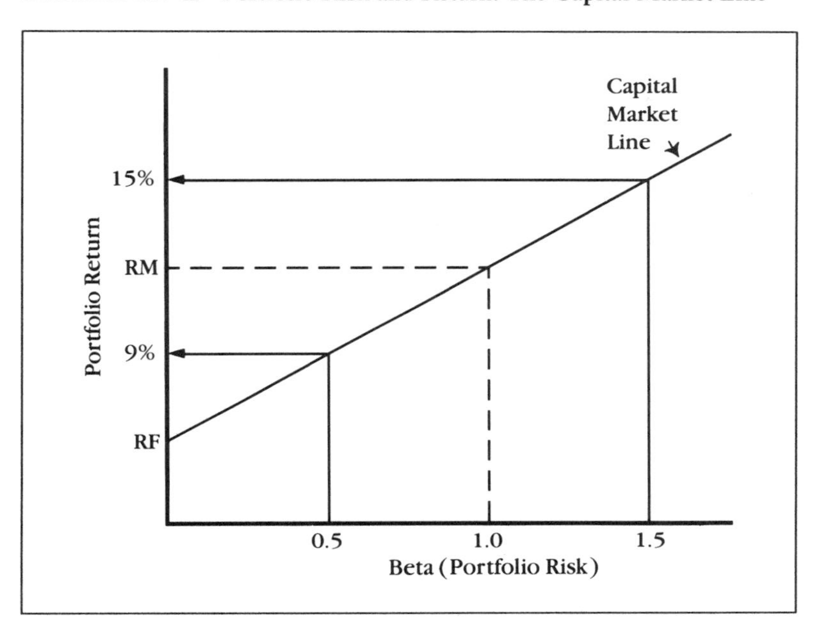

longed period, a portfolio whose beta is 1.2 could be expected to decline in value by approximately 60 percent. Of course, if stock prices were to rise by 50 percent, the value of this portfolio would climb by 60 percent.

Figure 8.2 illustrates the changes in quarterly returns for three funds: the Twentieth Century Ultra Fund (beta 1.40), the Vanguard 500 Index Portfolio (beta 1.00) and the Lindner Fund (beta 0.52). As you can see, the quarterly returns of the Ultra Fund, with its higher-than-average beta, are much more volatile than the returns of the other two funds. The Lindner Fund, with its lower-than-average beta, has been the least volatile of the three funds. It is important to note that beta does not distinguish a good fund from a poor one. It indicates only the extent to which a fund's shares will rise and fall, given changes in the overall stock market. Because investment return is linked to investment risk, high-beta funds tend to provide greater long-term returns than low-beta funds. However, whether you select a high-beta or low-beta fund depends on your personal preference.

FIGURE 8.2 □ Beta and Portfolio Volatility

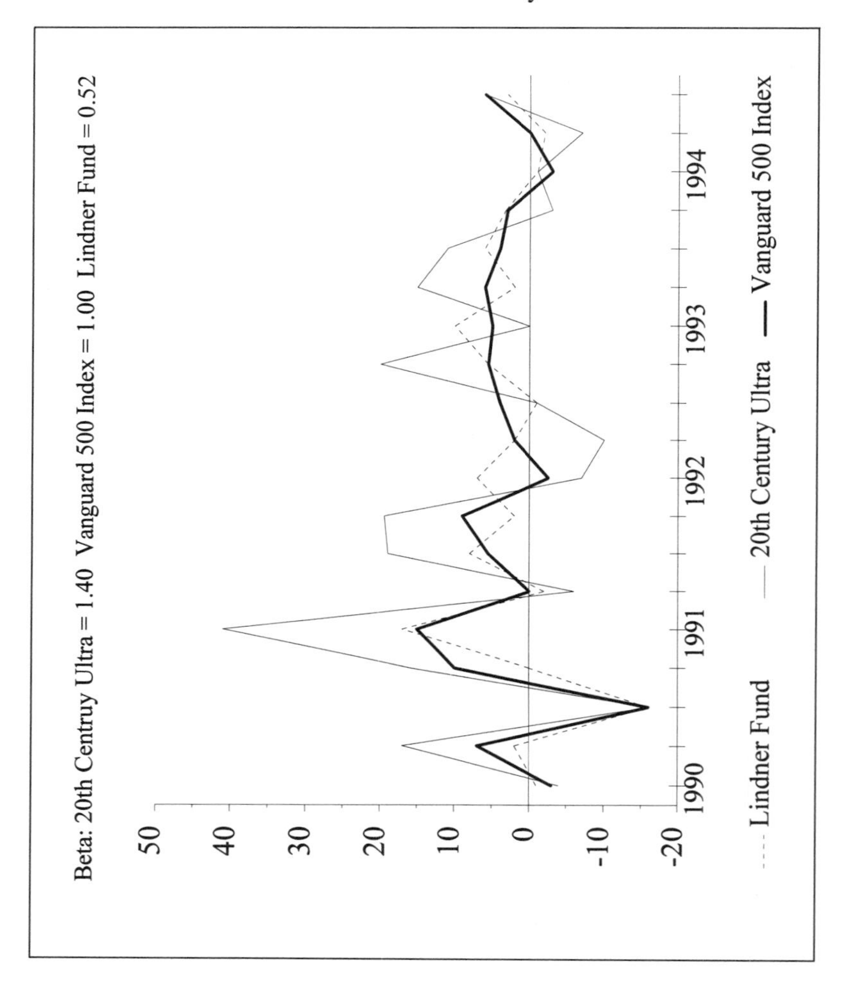

Remember, however, that beta provides a reliable risk index only for those funds that are well diversified. Portfolio risk is the sum of two components: market risk (systematic risk) and asset-specific risk (unsystematic risk). The typical common stock contains about one-third market risk and two-thirds asset-specific risk. On the other hand, the typical diversified growth mutual fund contains about 85 percent market risk and only about 15 percent asset-specific risk. In other words, diversifying eliminates nearly all asset-specific risk. As a result, fund volatility is reduced dramatically. In this case, 85 percent of the volatility of the fund's share price results from movements in the stock market.

Beta, however, is a good index of risk only for funds that are highly diversified. Funds that maintain concentrated portfolios, such as gold funds and industry sector funds, may be much riskier than indicated by their betas. That's because the lion's share of these funds' risk is asset specific or unsystematic. Because very little of their risk is related to the stock market, beta cannot indicate fund share price volatility. Rather than beta, most investors use the *standard deviation of return* to measure the risk inherent in equity funds that maintain concentrated portfolios. Fund statistical services such as *Morningstar* and *Value Line* provide standard deviations as well as fund betas. Although a discussion of standard deviation is beyond the scope of this presentation, you should know that, like beta, the greater a fund's standard deviation, the greater its share price volatility.

The importance of either beta or standard deviation is its reflection of an equity fund's risk. Knowing a fund's volatility allows you to build an investment portfolio that lies within your risk tolerance, or comfort zone. I have found that long-term-oriented investors earn higher returns than those who dip into and out of the stock market. While it is easy to maintain a long-term orientation as long as stock prices rise, many investors abandon this strategy at the first sign of a market downturn. Usually, such panic action occurs because the investors have assumed investment risk beyond their comfort zones. As a result, these investors often sell out at or near market bottoms and rarely participate in bull markets until much of the upward movement has already taken place. The result, generally, is suboptimal investment returns.

Fixed-Income Fund Risk

Bond fund investors in general are exposed to five types of risk: default risk, interest rate risk, maturity risk, liquidity risk and call risk. When lenders fail to make scheduled interest payments or repay principal, bonds go into default, and bond investors suffer either lost income or a decline in the value of the original loan. To a large measure, the portfolio diversification that bond funds provide limits the extent of default risk. Individuals who confine their investments to government bond funds or insured municipal bond funds eliminate this source of risk entirely.

Interest rate risk refers to the volatility of bond prices that results from changes in interest rates. The greater the changes in interest rates, the greater the changes in bond prices. Interest rate changes affect longer term bonds more than shorter term bonds.

When Interest Rates Increase by One Percentage Point

Average Maturity	*Price Change*
2 Years	–1.8%
10 Years	–6.4
25 Years	–9.9

When bond prices move in one direction or another, the volume of trading tends to increase. Bonds with rather limited markets can rise or fall in price by much more than bonds traded in active markets. Liquidity risk is lowest for actively traded Treasury bills and U.S. government bonds; it is highest for long-term maturity municipal bonds.

Finally, when interest rates fall, some bonds are called away from investors by the bonds' issuers. Bonds that possess a call provision therefore rise in price by far less than noncallable bonds during periods of declining interest rates. Furthermore, holders of callable bonds have their principal returned to them at the most inopportune time—when interest rates are generally at their lowest. In other words, callable bonds tend to be riskier than noncallable bonds, all other things being equal. In general, Treasury securities possess the least call risk, while call risk is greatest for municipal bonds and Ginnie Mae securities.

Unfortunately, most fixed-income investors ask what it pays when shopping for a bond fund. They often ignore both risk and the cost of investing in bond funds, but these two variables can wreak havoc with an income investor's long-run return. If you pay a sales commission to acquire a bond fund or ante up above-average annual expenses, your returns will surely suffer. If you invest in a bond fund that ranks on the high end of the risk spectrum, you may lose some of your hard-earned investment capital.

Most people would prefer to invest in a high-return, low-risk fund. Unfortunately, the financial world is not built that way. Investment return is nothing more than the reward you obtain for taking investment risks. If you want to earn any meaningful return at all, you must assume some investment risk. Alternatively, if a fund promises to produce a high rate of return, it most likely makes that promise because its portfolio manager will assume a relatively high degree of risk in pursuit of the return. Successful investors tend to be those who are aware of the risks as well as the rewards mutual funds provide, and these investors assume no more risk than they can reasonably tolerate.

9

Mutual Fund Trading Strategies

Over the long run, investment fundamentals determine the value of a share of common stock; that is, its long-term value is determined by such things as its earnings growth rate, return on equity, dividend yield and so on. In the short run, however, fear and greed can drive stock prices well above or below their fair values. Fear and greed also can cause financial disaster for investors who give in to these emotions. Fear can lead investors to park their money in "safe" money market funds, bank accounts or certificates of deposit. As the old adage goes, "It's better to be safe than sorry." After you pay taxes, however, money invested in these vehicles for long periods of time turns out to be unsafe after all. That's because inflation eats into this capital to such an extent that your investment wealth actually shrinks over time. And the longer money remains in these vehicles, the greater those losses become. On the other hand, greed can cause individuals to adopt investment postures that are so risky that setbacks can wipe out their nest eggs.

Some Basic Advice

So what can you do? The answer is simple: Don't give in to either emotion. Build a well-diversified portfolio that contains no more risk than you can tolerate, and vow to invest for the long term. Resolve to maintain that portfolio and gradually make changes as economic conditions warrant. This advice, of course, is easy to dispense, but hard to swallow. However, a review of historical stock market returns should increase your resolve to set aside your emotions when investing in mutual funds.

During the past 50 years, for example, common stocks—as represented by the Standard & Poor's 500 index—returned 12.9 percent compounded annually. If you had invested $1,000 in this portfolio at the beginning of 1942, it would have grown to $510,994 by the end of 1993. Of course, the value of that portfolio would have suffered some bumps and bruises along the way. During the 1973 to 1974 bear market, for example, the value would have tumbled more than 45 percent, and during the three months of September 1987 through November 1987, the value of the portfolio would have sunk by nearly 30 percent.

SMART STRATEGIES *Don't give in to fear or greed. Build a well-diversified portfolio holding only the risk you can tolerate, invest for the long term, maintain your portfolio and gradually make changes as economic conditions warrant.*

If you invest in the stock market, you will spend considerable time watching your portfolio value decline. In fact, since 1942, there have been 22 declines in stock prices of 8 percent or more, 18 decreases of 10 percent or more, 11 setbacks of 15 percent or more, 6 plunges of 20 percent or more and 3 declines exceeding 30 percent. During these declining periods, the stock market spent 171 months falling. In other words, during the past 50-plus years, the market has spent 30 percent of its time in retreat. These sharp market reversals have occurred, on average, every two and a half years. And these periods of decline have lasted from 1 to 21 months, with the average being 7.8 months.

Market Timing versus Buy-and-Hold Strategies

Market timers are quick to point out that they can help you maneuver the market's obstacle course and improve your investment returns. They mean that dodging bear markets can reduce portfolio volatility and enhance profits. This is a very powerful statement. It implies that market timers can both reduce risk and increase investment return. That, of course, is subject to considerable debate. In fact, many analysts believe that market timers expose investors to more risk than does a buy-and-hold strategy. The following example illustrates why.

I first identified the market's five best-performing and five worst-performing years since 1942. I then computed the value of investing $1, assuming an investor could dodge the worst-performing years. Of course, investment performance was enhanced. By dodging the market's worst-performing years, the value of $1 invested in 1942 would have grown to $1,098 by the end of 1993. That's a $597 improvement over a buy-and-hold strategy, or slightly more than twice the return of that passive strategy. On the other hand, a completely inept market timer who managed to stay *in* the market during the five *worst* years, but stayed *out* of the market during its five *best* years would have seen the value of $1 invested in 1942 increase to only $94 by the end of 1993. That's less than one-fiftieth of the value produced by a buy-and-hold strategy. In other words, you have more to lose by being absolutely wrong than you have to gain by being absolutely correct about the stock market's future direction.

Here are a few more examples: A market timer who happened to dodge the market's five worst years, but also stayed out of the market during its single best year would have attained a portfolio valued at $729, or about a 50 percent improvement over a buy-and-hold strategy. However, the investor who was out of the market during its five worst years, but missed two of its best years would not have kept pace with a buy-and-hold strategy. In other words, even if you make only a few timing errors, your long-run return will suffer.

If you were lucky enough to be out of the stock market during its five worst years (during the past 50), you would have increased your annual return from 12.7 percent (for a buy-and-hold strategy) to 14.6 percent. On the other hand, if you were unlucky and managed to be out of the market during its five best-performing years, your annual return would have been trimmed to 9.7 percent. So you have much more to lose by being out of the stock market than being in it.

Market timing *can* increase investment returns. However, even a few timing errors can cause investment returns to fall below those you can obtain with a passive buy-and-hold strategy. And the odds favor a reduction rather than an enhancement of portfolio value. In other words, attempting to time the market *increases* rather than *decreases* investment risk.

While it's painful to watch the value of your portfolio shrink during a bear market, it's better to stay the course than cut and run. As these examples have shown us, we have more to lose by missing a bull market than we have to gain by dodging a bear market. Bear markets are a fact of investment life, and you should learn to live with them. If you can't tolerate a severe market plunge, spread your capital around. For example, a portfolio containing one-third common stocks, one-third bonds and one-third money market mutual funds would have declined by less than 12 percent versus a 48 percent stock market decline during 1973 to 1974, the worst bear market in the past half-century.

Weighing the Value of Timing Services

Remember, the stock market is a highly efficient mechanism. This means that investment returns tend to parallel the risks you take. The ability of anyone to beat the market significantly without facing greater-than-average investment risk is nearly impossible. Although pockets of market inefficiencies do exist, investors who exploit them rarely add more than 2 to 3 percent annually to their overall investment portfolio returns. Thus, paying excessive fees to mutual fund timing services erodes nearly all the potential benefit you might obtain. In most cases, services that charge 2 percent or more annually are specifically designed to line the pockets of their promoters and not those of the mutual fund investor.

I do not suggest that all fees charged by investment advisers are unjustified. However, you should carefully consider the cost of investment advice as well as its potential benefit before you make a long-term commitment. Ask yourself how the cost affects the bottom line. If you believe that a mutual fund timing service is your cup of tea, avoid those that employ front-end load funds, invest in no-load funds and pay no more than 1 percent of the value of your portfolio annually for mutual fund investment advice.

Playing the Market by the Numbers—and Winning

Do you want to make a fortune in the stock market? It's simple: Buy low, and sell high. Many investors, however, take precisely the opposite approach to investing in equities. They buy high (when the financial world is full of optimism), and they sell low (after stock prices have plummeted and doomsayers ring the death knell for stocks). If you see a bit of yourself in this description, try dollar cost averaging.

Here's how and why dollar cost averaging works. Once you have selected an appropriate equity fund, you make periodic purchases in *equal dollar amounts.* For example, suppose you decide to invest $1,000 each quarter in your favorite fund. You buy the stock initially when its share price is $10. You buy the second time when its share price is $8; the third, $5; and the fourth, $10. (See Figure 9.1.) You have purchased a total of 525 shares at an average cost of $7.62 per share, while the average price during the period was $8.25. The reason, of course, is that you purchased more shares when share price was low and fewer shares when it was high. (You have solved half the problem of buying low and selling high.)

Dollar cost averaging your way into the stock market works best when you expect to constantly inject new capital into your invest-

FIGURE 9.1 □ Example of Dollar Cost Averaging in Action

Date	Share Price	Amount Invested	Shares Purchased
March 1992	$10	$1,000	100
June 1992	8	1,000	125
September 1992	5	1,000	200
December 1992	10	1,000	100
Total	$33	$4,000	525

Average Cost: 525 shares ÷ $4,000 = $7.62 per share
Average Price: $33 ÷ 4 = $8.25 per share

ment portfolio over a long period of time. Thus, this strategy appears especially attractive for IRA (individual retirement account) or pension plan investors or those saving for a child's education. Furthermore, if you want dollar cost averaging to work at all, you must invest in an asset whose price is highly variable, yet eventually heads to higher ground. This describes the typical equity mutual fund.

SMART STRATEGIES *Using a mutual fund's automatic investment plan (AIP) is one of the smartest, easiest and most convenient ways to build your investment nest egg.*

Beware of Drawbacks

While some market "experts" have touted dollar cost averaging as a foolproof way to make money trading stocks, the approach does have its drawbacks. First, if you dollar cost average a stock all the way down to zero, dollar cost averaging will not improve your return. Second, when the value of your portfolio towers over the amount of your regular investment, dollar cost averaging loses its impact. For example, if you hold 10,000 shares of a fund priced at

$10 per share, the next $1,000 investment amounts to only 1 percent of the portfolio's value ($100,000). Thus, that purchase will not significantly reduce your average cost. On the other hand, a $1,000 purchase made when portfolio value is $2,000 represents one-third of the portfolio's value. You can therefore achieve the greatest benefits from dollar cost averaging in the early stages of your investment program.

Also note that dollar cost averaging does not result in *automatic* investment gains and thus does not replace proper asset selection. As an investor, you still must determine how to allocate your assets and which funds you plan to use for your dollar cost averaging strategy. Finally, because dollar cost averaging requires regular purchases, it may not be suitable if your investment dollars are fixed (although you can use it when switching from one investment to another).

Enjoy the Advantages

These caveats aside, dollar cost averaging offers distinct advantages. First, the strategy allows you to spoon in your money in small amounts, so results do not depend on when you made the investment. (How many times does it seem as though you invested at the top?) Second, dollar cost averaging enables you to purchase more shares at lower prices and thus automatically lowers the average investment cost of a series of purchases. Third, it eliminates the emotional element of investing. You regularly inject new capital, regardless of extreme swings in the "mood" of the market—the times when people make the biggest investment mistakes. Finally, dollar cost averaging is highly compatible with a wealth-building program because you can make regular "installment" payments toward your financial independence.

Dollar cost averaging and mutual fund investing are highly compatible. Unlike individual stocks, diversified portfolios of mutual funds always head to higher ground. Thus, you are assured of increasing the average returns of your periodic investments. Also, mutual fund purchases are made in dollar amounts, not share amounts. Thus, unlike buying common stocks, you can purchase fractional shares of mutual funds. Finally, nearly every equity mutual fund offers a convenient automatic investment program. If you opt for automatic investment, you can make regular investments in your chosen funds, which withdraws the money automatically from your checking account. Automatic fund investing is one of the smartest, easiest and most convenient ways to build your investment nest egg.

Investing by Formula

Investors who bought and held stocks over the past ten years, despite some scary market corrections, realized sizable gains. In fact, investors who bought stocks at any time in this century and held them for 15 years would not have realized a loss. To some investors, this is a convincing argument for adopting a buy-and-hold strategy. However, to maintain a buy-and-hold strategy through thick and thin requires great intestinal fortitude. All too frequently, buy-and-hold investors find that the churning in the pits of their stomachs overcomes the rationality of staying the course. These investors usually dump their stocks at precisely the times that they should buy more—the depths of severe bear markets.

The surest way to garner the best profits in the stock market is to buy low and sell high. Easy to say, but hard to do. *Low* and *high* are relative terms. Thus, it's difficult, if not impossible, to know when stock prices are at their peaks or nadirs. But you have a way to profit from the stock market's inherent volatility while at the same time reducing the risk of your total investment portfolio. The strategy is called *formula investing.*

Formula investing is based on the simple idea that you take predetermined levels of profits in your aggressive investments and salt away the money in conservative investments such as money market funds or short-term bond funds. When stock prices decline, you switch some of your capital from these conservative investments back into the stock market. This way, you take profits when stock prices rise, and you use dollar cost averaging techniques when stock prices decline. Here's how one version of formula-investing (the constant dollar plan) works.

First, decide what parts of your capital to invest in equity funds and money market funds. For example, suppose that you decide to place $10,000 of your $20,000 investment in equity funds and the balance in money market funds. Next, you set the triggering points for when to switch between the two investment categories—say, a 20 percent increase or decrease in your equity portfolio. If the value of your initial commitment to equity funds ($10,000) rises to $12,000, for example, you would take the profits ($2,000) and switch them to your money fund, thus bringing your equity fund investments back to $10,000. If the value of your equity portfolio falls to $8,000, you would switch $2,000 from your money funds to your equity funds. Note that this approach requires that you sell after stock prices rise and that you buy after they decline, an automatic buy low, sell high strategy.

The trick with the constant dollar plan is to match your risk tolerance with the appropriate trigger. If you take profits too quickly, you could end up with too many trades and miss major market moves on the upside. In addition, unless the investments are in a tax-deferred savings plan like an IRA, you may pay premature taxes on your capital gains.

Although formula investing allows you to buy on market dips and to take profits during bull markets, it is not a get-rich-quick scheme. You must use it over several market cycles to succeed. The constant dollar tactic earns most in a market with a steep drop, in which you average down, followed by a resurgent bull. During a period when stock prices constantly move to higher ground, the constant dollar plan does well relative to a dollar cost averaging program split between stocks and money funds, but fails to beat a buy-and-hold strategy. In a sideways market, the performance might mimic that of a buy-and-hold strategy, but your after-tax return could be slightly lower if you were forced to do some switching and realized some capital gains on the transactions.

You also must choose the right type of aggressive equity fund to make formula investing work. Look for no-load aggressive equity funds that have posted sharp rebounds from their lows reached during previous market declines. Total return funds, or mutual funds that adjust their cash, stock and bond mixes generally produce inferior returns when used in formula investing because of their inherent conservatism. Aggressive funds that remain fully invested in the stock market allow you to maximize your profits on the upside and give you an opportunity to dollar cost average into the market on the downside. Thus, always examine a fund's investment strategy and its performance during up and down markets before using it in a formula plan.

One Lump or Several?

What is the best way to invest a large cash windfall? Although I have illustrated how dollar cost averaging can reduce the risk of investing cash received from a pension fund rollover or an inheritance, recent research indicates that dollar cost averaging may not be the best way to invest a large sum of cash in the stock market.

For example, take the poor fellow who received a lump-sum pension distribution in December of 1986 and spooned it into equity mutual funds during the next nine months. Shortly after he became fully invested, stock prices took a nosedive. In this case, spooning in cost this investor a bundle. Investing equal dollar amounts in the S&P 500 index in January, March, June and September would have resulted in a 9.8 percent decline in portfolio value by December 31, 1987. On the other hand, if he had invested the entire amount at the beginning of 1987, the portfolio's value would have increased by 5.2 percent by year-end. So much for reducing risk and increasing returns by easing into the market!

Furthermore, an examination of stock market returns during the past 50 years indicates that stock prices spend most of the time rising. During the past 50 years, stock prices were higher at the end of 36 years and lower at the end of 14 years. In other words, for any given year, you have a 72 percent chance that a gradual investment strategy will produce a return less than that of a lump-sum investment strategy. According to one study, the lump-sum strategy produced superior returns to three-month, six-month and one-year dollar cost averaging strategies, but *at higher levels of risk.* In short, long-term investors who are not concerned about the day-to-day or month-to-month gyrations in stock prices are better off investing lump sums immediately rather than spooning in a little at a time. Investors with shorter horizons who are risk averse should spoon in rather than invest a lump sum at one time. Although the break point between short term and long term is somewhat obscure, I suggest spooning in if you plan to withdraw your investment capital in five years or less, and investing a lump sum all at once if you look to withdraw more than five years in the future.

To see why lump-sum investing produces greater returns, let's compare the following examples. A $10,000 lump-sum investment made in early January of 1988 would have grown to $11,681 by year-end. Investing one-twelfth of this amount each month during 1988 would have produced a portfolio worth $10,968, a difference of $713. Assuming the stock market continues to produce an 11.8 percent average compound annual return (its historical average), this difference grows to $1,245 after five years, totals $2,175 after ten years and continues to widen as the investment holding period lengthens.

Of course, when stock market averages are hovering around their all-time record highs, it may not be the best time to dump a pile of cash into the stock market. However, if you are a long-term-oriented investor, getting on board immediately probably is better than waiting for a market correction. That's because being out of the market over the long run is worse than being in it. I know of a handful of investors who managed to dodge the October 1987 market crash. However, these cautious investors also were reluctant to jump back into the market after stock prices had plunged—some still have not waded back in. As a result, they are worse off than those investors who were in the market at the time of the crash and stayed the course.

Investing at Market Peaks

Four significant bear markets have occurred during the past quarter-century (1969–1970, 1973–1974, 1981–1982 and October–December 1987). If you had invested $10,000 at the market's peak shortly before the onset of each bear market, you would have invested a total of $40,000 at the worst times during the latter portion of this century. Within 12 months of each investment, the stock market would have posted a double-digit decline. However, by the end of 1993, your total investment would have grown more than sixfold. (See Figure 9.2.) In other words, making investments at the worst possible times still enables the long-term investor to pile up handsome profits.

FIGURE 9.2 □ An Investor's Worst Nightmare

Investment Date	Amount Invested	Market Decline	Portfolio Value 1993
December 1968	$10,000	–32.9%	$116,988
January 1973	10,000	–46.2	94,180
August 1981	10,000	–18.2	57,492
September 1987	10,000	–25.1	17,399
May 1990	10,000	–15.9	14,421
Totals	$50,000	—	$300,480

Although your emotions may tell you that it's not a good time to jump into the stock market, research indicates that investors who want to maximize their returns should not hold back capital earmarked for equity investments. When you think too much it's never a good time to invest in the stock market. After stock prices have risen substantially, valuations are high, and everyone begins to anticipate the impending market correction. After stock prices come crashing down, investors fear that prices will head even lower. As a result, most timid investors spend more time on the investment sidelines than they should. The result is predictable: lower long-term returns.

10

Managing Your Mutual Fund Portfolio

When should you sell? mutual fund investors frequently ask these days. But financial literature rarely addresses this question. Most of the mutual fund advice I have come across tends to focus on mutual fund selection criteria and does not fully discuss when to sell. To some extent, this is understandable because investing in a fund is tantamount to hiring an investment adviser, and you wouldn't want to change your investment adviser every month. In short, mutual funds are to buy and not to sell. Find a few good funds whose risk and return characteristics meet your current investment objectives and your risk tolerance requirements, and stick with those funds for the long term. More often than not, you will earn a better return than investors who hire and fire their portfolio managers at will.

I've never much liked market timing strategies, so I haven't spent a lot of time espousing active trading techniques. Admittedly, however, I know that there are times to be more fully invested in certain funds than others. In fact, the portfolio turnover rates of the portfolios I manage for individuals and pension funds have averaged about 30 percent during the past decade. In other words, I tend to turn over these portfolios completely about once every three years. Thus, while I tend to be a longer term investor, I don't marry my mutual fund selections for better or worse. At times, I trade them for other funds for a variety of reasons.

When To Bail Out

Unfortunately, I can give you very few hard and fast rules for determining when to sell a fund. ***In most cases, you should ask yourself why you invested in the fund in the first place. If that reason no longer applies, bail out.*** For example, suppose you invest in a government bond fund because it yields 10 percent, and you believe that interest rates are about to fall. Suppose further that, as you expected, the fund's yield declines to 6 percent, and you capture the lion's share of the fund's appreciation potential. Because rates have little room to fall further, the reason you bought the fund no longer is valid, and you should sell. Similarly, suppose you invest in an aggressive growth fund because you believe that the economy and corporate profits will expand at above-average rates. Instead, the economy weakens. Because the primary reason you bought the fund did not materialize, you should sell.

Ten More Reasons To Sell

1. **A fund manager who produced better-than-average returns relative to funds with similar objectives and investment strategies relinquishes the helm.** You may not wish to bail out immediately because it will take the new portfolio manager a while to restructure the fund. However, if you invested in the fund initially because of the portfolio manager's ability to perform well, consider selling the fund after that manager departs.
2. **A fund that has performed reasonably well changes its investment style.** This frequently happens to reasonably successful small-cap funds that attract a flood of new capital and are forced to invest in mid-cap rather than true small-cap stocks.
3. **A fund closes its doors to new investors.** Closing a fund to

new shareholders can eliminate one of the reasons for the fund's success (the ability to invest fresh cash in positions already held or to capitalize on new investment ideas). Once the fund closes, monitor its return closely. If performance begins to skid relative to like-kind funds, head for the exit.

4. **A fund's performance falls so that it is below average relative to its peers over a 12-month period.** Recent research indicates that a fund with a better-than-average performance record over a 12-month period has a high probability of continued success, while one with a relatively poor track record has a better-than-average chance of continuing its lackluster performance. Upgrade your investment to a similar fund whose 12-month performance ranks in the top third among its peers.
5. **An actively managed equity fund grows inordinately large.** For funds that invest in small-cap stocks, this threshold is about $400 million. For other equity funds, assets must swell beyond $1 billion.
6. **A period of declining interest rates forces a fund's yield below the yield on one-year Treasury bills plus 3 percent.** In this instance, the fund's interest rate risk does not justify its long-run return potential. Rarely do long-term bond yields fall far below this threshold during periods marked by low or modest rates of inflation.
7. **You wish to rebalance your overall portfolio.** For example, suppose you decide to maintain a 50-50 allocation to equity funds and bond funds. Rising stock prices cause the equity portion to increase to 70 percent. Therefore, you should sell some equity fund shares to rebalance the portfolio to its initial target.
8. **Your fund merges into another.** Usually, funds with poor long-term track records are absorbed by other funds. Most likely, you will have sold long before the merger is announced. If not, sell at once.
9. **You change your investment objectives.** This should not happen too often. However, review your personal financial circumstances at least once each year, and decide whether to stay the course or change the proportion of assets you

allocate to various categories of assets.

10. **You wish to spend some of your investment profits on the good things in life.** Remember, investing is not an end in itself. I have met too many people who believe that spending any of their investment capital is a cardinal sin. Frequently, these individuals suffer undue hardships because the income from their investments falls short of their preferred lifestyles, and they avoid selling any of their capital. Remember, the stock market over the long run has returned an average of nearly 12 percent annually. Thus, equity investors can withdraw up to 12 percent of their portfolios each year without ever depleting their nest eggs. In fact, with the differential tax rate on capital gains versus other income, it is better to withdraw 6 percent of your capital from an equity fund portfolio annually than to withdraw the interest from a "safe" bond fund with an interest yield of 6 percent.

Mutual funds are much different from individual securities. First, the diversification most mutual funds provide reduces investment risk significantly. Second, professional managers direct mutual fund portfolios. Third, funds generally stick with their mandated investment objectives and preferred investment styles. Thus, you have fewer reasons to sell a mutual fund than a specific stock or bond. However, there are times when you should sell. Do not become complacent about your mutual fund investments. Your investment portfolio should reflect the ongoing changes in personal circumstances, financial markets, the economy and the characteristics of individual funds.

Don't Sell for These Three Reasons

1. **You are afraid the stock market will take a nasty tumble.** Chances are you cannot see the future any better than anyone else. Remember, stock prices are always in a state of flux. In fact, stock prices spend about 30 percent of the time in retreat. If you can't stand the heat generated by falling stock prices, turn down the thermostat by allocating a

smaller portion of your assets to equities, and stick to this new comfort zone through thick and thin.

2. **The stock market has taken a nasty tumble, and you watch the value of your portfolio melt away.** At some point, you may throw up your hands in despair and decide to salvage what little you have left. This, of course, is the worst time to sell. Not only will you lock in your losses; you will most likely miss out on the ultimate market rebound, which is probably only moments away. Remember, bear markets usually hit bottom shortly after battered investors decide to throw in the towel.
3. **You have chalked up a handsome profit in one of your funds.** The problem with turning "paper" gains into "real" gains by selling your fund is that you usually have to share them with your Uncle Sam. Remember, whether realized or unrealized, gains still are profits. Premature payment of income taxes can easily clip 1 or 2 percent annually from your long-run investment return.

Are Foreign Investments Foreign to You?

Consider investing internationally for several reasons. First, as we saw in Chapter 4, investors who restrict their equity investments to U.S. stocks can miss out on explosive growth in other parts of the world. Although the United States experienced relatively strong economic growth during most of the 1980s, Japan did even better. It emerged from the decade as the dominant force in world trade and international banking. And Europe (especially unified Germany) could become the Japan of the 1990s. Although common stocks in the United States returned a hefty 17 percent each year during the 1980s, an index of European, Australian and Far East stocks (the EAFE index) grew by more than 22 percent annually during that decade.

While the possibility of earning above-average returns may be reason enough to include international stocks in your equity portfolio, you have an even more compelling reason to globally diversify your equity portfolio: The returns of foreign stocks and bonds rarely move in lock step with U.S. investment returns. Thus, you can somewhat offset losses in the value of U.S. stocks and bonds by gains in their foreign counterparts. In short, establishing a globally diverse portfolio reduces your risk without sacrificing your investment return.

The relatively low correlation between U.S. stock returns and foreign stock returns results from both the lead/lag relationships among world economies and fluctuating foreign exchange rates. Some academic studies indicate that the optimally balanced equity portfolio allocates from 30 percent to 50 percent of its assets to foreign stocks.

International investing, while highly attractive, has long posed problems for individual investors. Information on foreign companies is difficult to obtain. Furthermore, because of varying business customs and accounting standards, we cannot evaluate foreign companies with the same methods we use to evaluate the prospects and risks of U.S. companies. Finally, foreign stock investors incur political and foreign exchange risks that are largely absent from U.S. stock portfolios.

However, mutual funds that invest internationally solve many of the problems individuals face when investing in foreign stocks. Stock valuation and selection are left to professional management. Recordkeeping is simplified because dividend and interest payments are collected, converted to U.S. dollars and paid to shareholders in a single payment. Finally, mutual funds are highly diversified, thereby reducing some of the risks of investing internationally.

Although international mutual fund investing remains in its infancy, more than 100 funds invest internationally. Today, you can find international funds that invest in money market instruments (Fidelity Spartan and Dreyfus World Wide, for example); bonds (Scudder International Bond Fund and T. Rowe Price International Bond Fund); small-firm stocks (Dimensional Fund Advisors Small Cap Japan Fund); and even selected industries (GT Global Health Fund). Because investing overseas continues to grow, expect to see the organization of numerous international funds in the next few years. These new funds will greatly increase return potential for individual investors who opt to globally diversify their stock and bond portfolios.

Fund Alternatives for Income-Oriented Investors

If your certificate of deposit (CD) is due to mature soon, you will probably be shocked by the yields available in the bond market these days. Gone are the heady days when high-quality debt instruments sported double-digit yields. The fact is, double-digit yields prevailed for so long that most income-oriented investors forgot their bond market history lesson and grew spoiled by the handsome yields offered during most of the past decade.

Figure 10.1 lists the average returns and average yields for long-term government bonds during each of the past five decades. As you can see, only the 1980s provided average double-digit bond yields and total returns. In fact, for most of the past half-century, bond yields rose. As a result, holders of long-term bonds fared very poorly (except in the 1980s). On average, the total annual return for long-term government bonds during the past half-century stands at a paltry 4.5 percent. And corporate bond investors fared only slightly better with a 4.9 percent average annual return. Note also that the total average returns for long-term government bonds failed to keep pace with the rates of inflation during the 1940s, 1950s, 1960s and 1970s.

So what's a fixed-income investor to do? You have three alternatives: you can live with the yields available; you can both stretch the maturities of your portfolios and lower the quality of your

FIGURE 10.1 □ Long-Term Government Bond Yields and Total Returns

Decade	Annual Return	Average Yield	Inflation
1940s	3.2%	2.3%	5.4%
1950s	–0.1	3.4	2.2
1960s	1.4	5.4	2.5
1970s	5.5	7.3	7.4
1980s	12.6	10.6	5.1

investments; or you can combine equities with bonds in an attempt to boost your total return.

Most people living on fixed incomes can ill afford to pare their budgets any further. Thus, an investor with $250,000 invested in a CD yielding 10 percent and receiving $25,000 annually will be hard pressed to roll over that investment into another CD yielding 7 percent and paying $17,500 annually. Furthermore, most fixed-income investors cannot afford to assume the risk that accompanies double-digit bond yields these days. Thus, I suggest that income-oriented investors combine equity fund investments with bond fund and/or money fund investments to boost total return.

While the prices of equity funds are subject to the whims of the marketplace, funds that invest in stocks with higher-than-average dividend yields possess about 60 percent of the risk present in the typical growth fund. Furthermore, over the long run, companies that pay cash dividends tend to share their growth with investors by boosting cash dividends. Thus, unlike a long-term bond that pays a fixed amount annually, a diversified portfolio of dividend-paying stocks provides a significant inflation hedge because of increased annual payouts. For example, if a stock has a 6 percent dividend yield that increases by 5 percent annually, the payout doubles after 14 years, and based on the initial purchase price, so does the yield. As a bonus, the stock price usually rises along with the dividend. Thus, not only do investors receive more annual income, the value of their principal expands along with consumer prices.

Here's one suggestion: Create a portfolio consisting of 50 percent government or investment-grade bond funds and 50 percent yield-oriented equity funds. (These equity funds include balanced funds, value funds, growth and income funds, utility funds and convertible bond funds.) You can expect that portfolio to provide a long-term total annual return of about 10 percent.

Figure 10.2 lists equity funds that tend to provide higher-than-average dividend yields. While the returns of these funds have been nothing to write home about in recent years, they use very conservative investment strategies and thus are low-risk equity funds. Most have betas of less than half that of the typical equity fund.

FIGURE 10.2 □ Equity Funds that Contain Higher-than-Average Dividend Yields

Fund Name	Policy
Growth & Income	
Bartlett Basic Value	Value Stocks
Dodge & Cox Balanced	Balanced
Dodge & Cox Stock	Value Stocks
Dreyfus Fund	Flexible
Evergreen Total Return	Balanced
Fidelity Balanced	Balanced
Fidelity Equity Income	Divid. Stocks
Fidelity Puritan	Balanced
Financial Industrial Income	Divid. Stocks
Founders Equity Income	Divid. Stocks
Lindner Dividend	Balanced
Lindner Fund	Divid. Stocks
Price Equity Income	Divid. Stocks
Price Growth & Income	Flexible
SAFECO Income	Balanced
Scudder Growth & Income	Divid. Stocks
Stratton Monthly Div. Shares	Flexible
Strong Total Return	Flexible
Value Line Income	Balanced
Vanguard Star	Flexible
Vanguard Wellesley Income	Balanced
Vanguard Wellington	Divid. Stocks
Sector Funds	
Financial Strategic Utilities	Utilities
Flag Telephone Income	Telephone
Franklin Utilities	Utilities
Convertible Bonds	
Fidelity Convertible Sec.	Conv. Bonds
Value Line Convertible	Conv. Bonds
Vanguard Convertible	Conv. Bonds

Granddaddy Funds

Excluding money market funds, more than 4,000 mutual funds have appeared on the scene during the past dozen years. Not only has the number of funds expanded significantly, so has their variety. In addition to "plain vanilla" funds (diversified growth, growth and income, and aggressive growth funds), you can invest in international equity funds (global, regional or country specific), international bond funds, sector funds, small-cap funds, leveraged funds, domestic bond funds of all types, asset allocation funds and others.

If you discovered mutual funds only recently, you may be surprised to find that they have been around for a long time (see Figure 10.3). In fact, I counted more than 60 funds whose histories stretch back more than 50 years. A dozen funds initiated before the Great Crash of 1929 still operate. And one fund, the Colonial Fund, has been around since 1904. Most of these graybeards offer staid investment strategies. A large number are *balanced funds* (i.e., invest in a fixed ratio of stocks and bonds), a few are bond funds and the balance invest in dividend-paying common stocks (equity income funds) or seek growth of capital by pursuing plain vanilla asset selection strategies. A sales load of some kind accompanies most of these funds. That's the way funds were sold a half-century ago.

Mix, Don't Match—Diversify

All investors should practice diversification. It reduces risk. And believe it or not, diversification does not decrease long-run rates of return. Investors who hold portfolios of 30 or 40 stocks are exposed to about one-third the variability of return as investors who hold three or four stocks. This is because stocks that increase in price tend to offset those that decrease in price.

The mutual fund industry has thrived on the benefits of diversification. During the past decade, millions of investors discovered the risk-reduction benefits of mutual funds and poured billions of dollars into stock and bond funds. And the mutual fund industry

FIGURE 10.3 □ Granddaddy Funds

Fund Name	Year Began	Policy
Alliance Balanced Shares	1932	Balanced
Alliance Fund	1938	Common Stock
Alliance Growth & Income	1932	Common Stock
American Balanced	1932	Balanced
American Fund Inv.	1932	Common Stock
American Invest. Co. Amer.	1933	Common Stock
Century Shares Trust	1928	Specialized
Colonial	1904	Common Stock
Composite Bond & Stock	1939	Balanced
Delaware Fund	1938	Common Stock
Dodge & Cox Balanced	1931	Balanced
Eaton Vance Investors	1932	Flexible
Federated Stock & Bond	1934	Balanced
Financial Industrial	1935	Common Stock
Founders Blue Chip	1938	Common Stock
Franklin Equity	1933	Common Stock
IDS Mutual	1940	Balanced
Mass. Investors Growth	1932	Common Stock
Mass. Investors Trust	1924	Common Stock
National Bond	1940	Bond
Nationwide	1933	Flexible
Nicholas Income	1924	Flexible
Pilgrim High Yield	1938	Bond
Pioneer Fund	1928	Common Stock
Putnam, George, Fund	1937	Balanced
Putnam Investors	1925	Common Stock
SAFECO Equity	1932	Common Stock
Scudder Growth & Income	1929	Common Stock
Scudder Income	1928	Bond
Selected Amer. Shares	1933	Common Stock
Seligman Common Stock	1929	Common Stock
Seligman Growth	1937	Common Stock
Sentinel Balanced	1938	Balanced
Sentinel Common Stock	1933	Common Stock
Sovereign Investors	1936	Common Stock
USF&G Axe-Houghton Fund B	1938	Balanced
USF&G Axe-Houghton Growth	1932	Common Stock
USF&G Axe-Houghton Income	1938	Flexible
Vanguard Wellington	1929	Balanced

accommodated these eager investors by bringing to market mutual funds hosting nearly every investment strategy imaginable.

The plethora of new funds, accompanied by intensive hype, gave rise to a new breed of mutual fund investor—the mutual fund investment "junkie." Such investors are addicted to mutual funds. They buy funds listed in the *Forbes* "Honor Roll," funds touted in *Money* magazine, funds that score high in recent performance ratings published by *Barron's* and other financial newspapers and funds recommended in mutual fund advisory newsletters. The result? Each mutual fund junkie owns dozens of funds. Generally, they give little consideration to the compatibility of their funds. And this can cause serious problems for these investors.

You might think: "If some diversification is good, a lot of diversification must be better." To some extent, this statement is true. However, diversification has its limits. If you hold 1,000 stocks, you are exposed to about the same degree of risk as an investor who holds 200 stocks. Because the typical equity fund holds about 100 stocks, an investor who holds ten funds drawn from a single investment category (e.g., growth or aggressive growth) is exposed to about the same degree of risk as an investor who holds one or two funds. Furthermore, funds with similar investment objectives tend to hold similar common stocks. And owning shares of Philip Morris, for instance, in a half-dozen portfolios can result in redundant transactions costs that reduce overall investment return.

For example, suppose you own two funds that invest in large-company, blue chip stocks. Assume that both funds hold Philip Morris common stock. One fund manager decides to add another 100,000 shares of the stock, while the other decides to reduce his or her investment by 100,000 shares. Therefore, even though *your* portfolio is unchanged, as a fund shareholder you assumed the costs of both trades. Multiply this example by dozens of stocks, and redundant transactions costs begin to mount.

A few years ago, I assembled a random sample of 16 growth funds that invest in large-firm, blue chip stocks and examined the 25 largest holdings listed in each fund's most recent annual or semiannual shareholders' report. Of these 400 top investments, 112 appeared in more than one fund's portfolio. Fifteen stocks turned up in four or more fund portfolios, and the most popular holding appeared in 10 of the 16 portfolios.

Remember, I obtained these results by focusing on each fund's largest investments, which accounted for about one-half of each fund's total assets. On average, each of these funds held about 100 stocks. Thus, if I had used the entire list of each fund's holdings, the number of redundant stocks would have expanded greatly.

While most mutual funds pay only a few cents a share in brokerage commissions to trade stocks when they buy or sell, payment of a market maker's bid-ask spread and the large blocks of shares distort existing market prices—they bid up prices when they buy and cause prices to decline when they sell. A large block trade can add several hundred basis points to a round-up trade. For example, the total cost of a round-trip trade for a $250,000 block of stock averages about 3 percent. Given that blue chip stocks have returned an average of about 12 percent annually during the past six decades, redundant investments could clip long-run investment return by 1 or 2 percent annually. While this appears to be a trivial amount, I assure you it is not. For instance, the difference between a $10,000 investment that earns 11 percent and one that earns 12 percent over a 20-year period amounts to slightly more than $15,800!

How To Mix

This aside, I believe that you should invest in more than one mutual fund. However, I recommend that you make diverse selections to minimize portfolio duplication and the excess costs that often result. The simplest way to avoid duplication is to invest in different categories of funds. For example, an aggressive growth fund that focuses on rapidly growing companies with equity capitalizations of less than $300 million will have virtually no investments in common with a growth fund that invests in large-cap, blue chip stocks.

A second way to avoid duplication is to invest in funds drawn from the same category (e.g., aggressive growth or growth), but having different management styles. For instance, a fund whose management seeks high-growth companies that possess earnings momentum will most likely share very few investments with a fund whose management seeks "value" investments among industries and companies that are "out of favor." The former portfolio will most likely consist of stocks with high PE (price-earnings) ratios, while the latter will hold low-PE-ratio stocks, or even stocks of companies with no earnings at all (i.e., potential turnaround situations).

S MART STRATEGIES *Invest in more than one fund, but vary the types of funds to minimize portfolio duplication and reduce transactions costs.*

Diversification across investment styles makes good sense. First, you avoid portfolio duplication. Second, investment styles come into and go out of vogue during various phases of the market cycle. By investing in funds with different styles of management, you avoid the near-impossible task of determining which style is the next to become hot. Furthermore, using this diversification strategy increases the odds that your long-run returns will equal the risks you have assumed.

Count Your Funds

Here are a few suggestions for maintaining a slimmed down, yet appropriately diversified portfolio of mutual funds. Because the appropriate number of mutual funds to hold depends on your objective, I have based my recommendations on four investment strategies: growth, growth and income, income, and asset allocation.

Growth If you are a growth investor with a long investment horizon, seek primarily capital appreciation, and disregard the stock market's short-term swings. This implies a portfolio dominated by equity funds. However, given that blue chip stocks, small-cap stocks and international equities exhibit returns that are less than perfectly correlated with one another, you can reduce risk by including all three categories of funds in your growth-oriented portfolio. As a consequence, proper diversification requires that you spread your investments across five or six equity funds in addition to a money market fund, which can be used to park temporary cash. These funds should include small-cap growth, small-cap value, large-cap growth, large-cap value and international equity funds and perhaps a specialty fund such as a regional international fund or an industry sector fund.

Growth and income Because of your desire for current income, as a growth and income investor, you should define your portfolio more narrowly than would a growth investor. Typically, growth and income investors hold both conservative (income-producing) stock funds and bond funds. Your recommended portfolio should include a balanced fund, an equity income fund, a large-cap value fund and perhaps two bond funds (a corporate and a government bond fund). Including a money market fund, the ideal growth and income portfolio contains five or six funds.

Income Because bond fund returns tend to be much more highly correlated with one another, if you are an income-seeking investor, you need to hold fewer funds than the growth-seeking investor. However, you should diversify your portfolio among corporate, government and international bond funds. Including a money market fund brings the optimal total to four funds.

Asset allocation Asset allocators attempt to minimize forecasting errors by investing in many categories of assets. Your goal is to produce a low-variability portfolio. I recommend that you—as an asset allocator—invest in funds drawn from seven asset categories, including small-cap stocks, blue chip stocks, domestic bonds, international bonds, international stocks, gold, and money market funds. In addition, divide your small-cap and large-cap investments between value and growth funds and your domestic bond funds among corporate and government. Thus, you can hold as many as a dozen funds without having to worry about the return erosion that occurs when investments overlap.

Avoid becoming a mutual fund junkie. Establish concrete investment objectives, and invest in only those funds that make a meaningful contribution to your long-range plan. Eliminate redundancy and increase your return potential by investing in an appropriate number of mutual funds. Periodically, audit your mutual fund portfolio. Classify each fund by investment objective and management style, and eliminate those whose objectives and styles overlap. When choosing a new fund, determine which fund you will sell to accommodate the new purchase. This advice will help you increase both the efficiency and long-run return potential of your mutual fund portfolio.

Are Index Funds Your Cup of Tea?

Indexing, once considered a mere hedging device, has come into its own. Increasingly, investors turn away from actively managed portfolios for the assurance of market-level returns index funds offer. Of the pension funds surveyed by *Institutional Investor* in 1991, nearly 40 percent used a passive investment strategy for more than 25 percent of their equity and fixed-income assets. In turn, the number of index mutual funds has grown to more than 50 since 1974, when the first index vehicle debuted. Simultaneously, index fund assets have swelled beyond $20 billion. Whereas the original index funds tracked the S&P 500, the universe of index funds has since expanded to encompass an array of market segments, including the Dow Jones Industrial Average, the Wilshire 4500, the Russell 2000, the Morgan Stanley Europacific Index and the Salomon Brothers Broad Investment-Grade Bond Index. (See Figure 10.4.)

Why has indexing—the investment approach that seeks to parallel the investment returns of a particular stock or bond market segment (or index)—gained such popularity? The answer has its roots in both theory and practice. The concept of indexing was pioneered in the mid-1970s as a logical response to the efficient market theory (EMH), which proposed that the stock and bond markets work so efficiently that it is virtually impossible to beat the broad averages. If you can't beat the market, buy it, say proponents of EMH. Forget about picking stocks. Even for those who question the validity of this theory, the case for indexing is difficult to refute. Over long periods of time, the broad stock market averages have outperformed the majority of actively managed portfolios. Of the nearly 500 stock mutual funds in existence, fewer than 10 percent beat the unmanaged S&P 500 index over the past ten years, after

FIGURE 10.4 □ Index Funds

Fund Name	Index	Year Started
Benham Gold	North Amer. Gold Equities Index	1988
Colonial Int'l Equities	EAFE	1986
Colonial Small Stock	Smallest 20% NYSE	1986
Colonial U.S. Equities	S&P 500	1986
Dreyfus People's Index	S&P 500	1990
Fidelity Spartan Market Index	S&P 500	1988
Gateway Index	S&P 500	1977
Portico Equity Index	S&P 500	1990
Rushmore OTC Index Plus	S$P 500	1985
Rushmore Stock	Nasdaq 100	1985
Vanguard Bond Market	Salomon Bros. Inv. Gr.	1986
Vanguard Index Trust: Extended	Wilshire 4500	1987
Vanguard Index Trust: 500	S&P 500	1976
Vanguard Int'l Index: Europe	Morgan Stanley Europe	1990
Vanguard Int'l Index: Pacific	Morgan Stanley Pacific	1990

adjusting for sales charges. As the task of beating the market becomes increasingly difficult—if not impossible—for active portfolio managers, more and more investors find themselves attracted to the benefits of indexing.

Advantages

To be sure, the benefits of indexing are irrefutable. First and foremost, an index portfolio offers highly predictable results in line with its benchmark every year. While you have no guarantee of superior results, you can feel assured that your fund will not seriously underperform the averages. Moreover, an index—or a passive—strategy involves substantially lower costs than active portfolio management. Low portfolio turnover keeps transactions costs minimal, while low trading and minimal research needs often allow fund sponsors to waive all or a portion of the management fee. The benefits of low transactions costs are particularly significant in the small-company sector, where trading costs run very high.

Beware of Drawbacks

Of course, passive investment strategies have some drawbacks. For starters, the market doesn't always rise. As Vanguard carefully notes in its pamphlet, "Some Plain Talk about Indexing," index funds stay 100 percent invested at all times, whereas actively managed portfolios often hold at least some cash. In the prolonged bull market of recent years, index funds' fully invested stance worked to their advantage, while cash reserves slowed the returns of many actively managed portfolios. But just as index funds can be expected to closely track market rallies, so, too, will they fully participate in market declines.

Of course, not all index funds are alike. Substantial differences exist, even among funds that mirror the same index. Such funds can vary with respect to the manner in which they construct their portfolios. Are they pure-index or quasi-index vehicles? A pure-index vehicle attempts to replicate exactly the performance characteristics of its benchmark. It invests in every stock in its respective index, weighing each one according to its market capitalization. In contrast, a quasi-index vehicle strives to achieve results relatively in line with its benchmark by investing in a representative sample of the index's stocks. Still other funds, often identifiable by the "plus" in their names, attempt to enhance the returns available from a passively constructed portfolio by using derivative instruments (i.e., stock index futures and options). Despite their names, such funds generally subtract value, due to both the high costs associated with options strategies and the impact of derivative instruments on a fund's market exposure.

Both the impact of costs on a fund's ability to produce returns in line with its benchmark index and the narrow range of returns available from different index funds with the same objective make the degree to which a fund succeeds in minimizing transactions and operating costs critical. All else being equal, the lower a fund's costs, the better its chances of meeting its objective. Because one of the key advantages of indexing is reduced costs, an index fund with high expenses and/or sales charges is a contradiction in terms. If you opt for the index route, limit your selections to funds with relatively low expense ratios.

Up to this point, I have provided you with the tools you will need to implement your lifetime investment program. However, as any good carpenter knows, a well-delineated blueprint is a requisite for a successful project. In the next chapter, I outline several investing blueprints for varying investment objectives. Study these blueprints carefully before you dip into your mutual fund investing tool kit.

11

Wealth Building for Life

When selecting equity mutual funds, a vast majority of investors focus on past returns. Funds that have been top performers during some previous time period usually get the nod. However, investors don't agree about what time period they should use to judge a fund's relative performance. Some investors require that their selections be among the top performers over a three-year to five-year period. Others focus exclusively on the short run and select those funds that have performed well for a single quarter or two.

If equity markets are efficient, however, you have to question whether you should even use the historical return-based mutual fund selection model. In an efficient market, investment return is solely a function of investment risk. To obtain greater potential returns, you must opt for higher risk portfolios. In an efficient market, you can gain no advantage over other investors by investing in undervalued stocks or by attempting to time the market.

Even if the stock market works efficiently, however, do not blindly select mutual funds by throwing darts at the financial page or by using some other random-selection method. You still must match your investment portfolio with your return requirements and your tolerance for investment risk. (For example, if you are conservative, seek funds that have lower-than-average volatility.) Furthermore, you generally can improve your long-run rates of return by reducing the costs of investing. Thus, when making your final selections, opt for the lowest cost funds that meet your risk and return requirements.

Finally, a growing body of research indicates that the largest portion of investment return is determined by asset allocation decisions—that is, the categories of investments selected and the percentage of capital allocated to each category. Given the importance of asset allocation decisions, they should be your top priority. Once you make these decisions, choose the best funds available in each category. However, very little research exists regarding individual fund selection and investment return. As a result, investors tend to hang their hats on past performance.

Interestingly, recent research indicates that investors who select funds whose managers recently have had hot hands may have a profitable selection strategy. One important study that focused on 165 aggressive growth, growth, and growth and income funds between 1974 and 1988 indicates that using past returns to select equity funds can produce above-average returns. Investor portfolios exhibited a degree of performance momentum that should not exist in an efficient market. That is, the better performing portfolios continued to deliver better-than-average performance, while the poor performers continued to deliver subpar returns. In addition, the study found that investors should not arbitrarily select a time frame in which to judge a fund's relative historical performance. The best results occurred when investors constructed their portfolios by ranking funds on the basis of performance over a 12-month period. After adjusting the returns of all portfolios for risk, the study found that the portfolio containing the best historical performers (the top 12.5 percent of funds ranked from best to worst performers during the previous 12 months) returned about 4 percent per year more than it should have, and the portfolio containing the poorest historical performers (bottom 12.5 percent) returned about 4 percent per year *less* than it should have.

Therefore, the study indicates that you can improve your portfolio's returns by seeking the best performing funds over the previous 12 months and avoiding those with relatively poor performance over the same period. Revise your portfolio periodically by purging those funds that have cooled and adding those funds that have risen to the top of the performance charts.

While this is exciting news, note that a strategy based on the results of this study will increase portfolio turnover significantly. Thus, the use of no-load funds is essential. If you pay a 3 or 4 percent sales commission (either on the front end or the back end), you erase nearly all of the potential extra returns. Also, switching from one no-load fund to another can be costly because of the time lag between receiving your capital from one fund and investing it in another. For example, assume that it takes two weeks to make the switch. During these two weeks, your investment return is zero. If you turn over your entire mutual fund portfolio twice each year, you get four weeks of downtime, during which your capital is idle. Because the typical equity mutual fund returns about 12 percent each year, expect to trim about 100 *basis points* (one percentage point) from your total return (one basis point equals 0.01 percent). Thus, the potential extra average annual return decreases from 4 percent to 3 percent.

SMART STRATEGIES *Investors can improve their performance by seeking the best-performing funds over the previous 12 months.*

Finally, remember that most of your eventual long-run portfolio return will be determined by asset allocation. For example, suppose you make equal allocations to equity, bond and money market funds. The hot-hands strategy (adjusted for idle time) can add about 100 basis points to your total portfolio return. However, an extra 1 percent each year is not a small amount. If, for instance, you invest $10,000 and earn 10 percent annually for 20 years, your portfolio will grow to $67,270. If you invest the same amount for the same period and earn 11 percent, your portfolio expands to $80,620—an improvement of $13,350.

Don't Set Unrealistic Return Expectations or Build Castles in the Air

After more than a decade of exceptional returns, many investors now seeking riches in the stock market are building castles in the air. It's time for a reality check.

During the past few years, my mailbox has been crammed with direct-mail marketing packages sent by investment gurus promising to make me rich. Some guarantee "safe" returns of 15 to 20 percent each year. Others claim that their systems have produced returns of 30 percent or more. One brazened adviser boasted a 390,900 percent total return between 1980 and 1992. That's an astounding 89 percent compound annual return. A direct-mail marketing specialist told me recently that you can't expect to get many people to subscribe to an investment advisory newsletter unless you promise to provide annual returns in excess of 20 percent.

No doubt many self-appointed investment gurus have "earned" average annual returns exceeding 20 percent in recent years. That hasn't been too hard to do considering that an average-risk equity portfolio such as the Standard & Poor's 500 Index "returned" more than 15 percent during the entire decade of the 1980s. I even counted 72 mutual funds that have posted 20-plus percent annual returns during the five years ending December 1993. That's one out of every 20 funds that have been around that long. Invest $10,000 today, earn 20 percent annually, and 26 years later, your portfolio will be worth $1,144,000. If becoming a millionaire were only that easy.

Figure 11.1 lists the modern-day investment returns of a wide array of investments, along with a risk index called *standard deviation.* (Remember, the greater the standard deviation, the greater is portfolio volatility or risk.) The one thing you should notice immediately is that no category of investment has returned an average of 20 percent annually during the past half-century. Emerging market stocks, the top-performing asset category, returned an average of 16 percent each year since 1945. Also note that the categories producing the highest returns were those with the highest risk indexes. Finally, notice that Treasury bills, the lowest risk asset category, has produced almost no meaningful return at all. After adjusting

FIGURE 11.1 □ Annual Rates of Return 1945–1992

	Annual Return	Inflation-Adjusted Annual Return	Standard Deviation
Emerging Market Equities	16.9%	12.5%	25.8%
Venture Capital	15.9	11.5	25.5
Japanese Stocks	15.8	11.4	29.1
Emerging Growth Stocks	13.7	9.3	25.8
Small-Cap Stocks	13.6	9.2	25.5
E.A.F.E. Index	13.2	8.8	26.8
S&P 500 Index	11.7	7.3	16.3
U.S. Farmland	9.8	5.4	7.4
Art	8.7	4.3	14.5
Real Estate (Commercial)	7.2	2.8	5.8
Real Estate (Residential)	7.2	2.8	4.0
Corporate Bonds	5.6	1.2	9.7
Long-Term Government Bonds	5.1	0.7	9.7
Gold Bullion	5.1	0.7	25.8
Treasury Bills	4.8	0.4	3.2
Silver Bullion	4.9	0.5	55.8
Inflation	4.4	—	—

T-bill returns for inflation, their annual real (after inflation) return falls to a meager 0.30 percent each year.

Remember, these are the returns of hypothetical portfolios and thus have not been adjusted for transactions costs or income taxes, which affect all investors' returns. Take the hypothetical portfolio of large-cap, blue chip stocks as represented by the Standard & Poor's 500 Index, for example. If, as an active trader, you turn over this portfolio once a year and pay a 1 percent brokerage commission to buy stocks and 1 percent to sell them, the after-transactions-cost annual return falls from 11.7 percent to 9.7 percent. If you apply a 28 percent tax rate to these investment profits, the portfolio's *net* average annual return falls to 7 percent. Deduct the annual rate of inflation from this return, and you get a 2.5 percent net real return. At this rate of return, it would take 187 years for a $10,000 investment to grow to $1 million.

If you believe that you will earn 30 percent or more annually from your investment portfolio, you are being highly unrealistic. During his 15-year tenure at the helm of the Fidelity Magellan Fund, Peter Lynch produced a 30.5 percent average annual return. However, chances are you're no Peter Lynch. Furthermore, both history and financial theory will tell you that anyone who promises a "safe" 30 percent average annual return is lying. Of the 140 investment newsletters tracked by Mark Hulbert, editor of *The Hulbert Financial Digest,* the top performer (the *Value Line Investment Survey*'s portfolio of number-one-ranked stocks) returned 18.5 percent annually during the 13 years Hulbert has been in business. (Hulbert adjusts portfolio returns for brokerage commissions, but ignores the impact of income taxes.) Take a hint from history. If the high-risk equities return an average of 16 percent each year, the only way you will earn more is to assume even greater risks. And if you do, you increase the odds that your hard-earned bankroll will eventually disappear.

I'm sure that the next couple of decades will produce a slew of disappointed investors. The returns of the past dozen years have been anything but normal. Blue chip stocks have returned an average of more than 16 percent each year since the latest great bull market took off in late 1982. Bond investors have been treated to double-digit returns as well. Long-term government bonds, for example, returned an average of slightly less than 15 percent each year from late 1982 through early 1994. Even the most conservative investors who parked their capital in Treasury bills, money market funds or bank certificates of deposit reaped abnormally high returns during that period. During the ten years ending December 31, 1993, T-bills returned an average of 7 percent annually, or 3 percent more than the rate of inflation.

Whenever investment returns stray above or below their long-run averages for a prolonged period of time, they tend to reverse course for an extended period of time as well. Chances are both blue chip stocks and long-term bonds will provide returns far below their long-run averages for the remainder of this decade. Small-cap stocks, underperformers for most of the 1980s, will most likely surge. The same is probably true of gold and silver bullion. However, these predictions are far from sure bets. In short, don't expect to continue to earn the high returns that financial assets have provided during the past decade or so, and don't believe anyone who tells you otherwise.

While some investors surely will suffer because they have built castles in the air, many others have adopted such conservative postures that they have little chance of earning any meaningful return at all. I recently examined the more than $2 trillion now invested in mutual funds. I found that money market mutual funds account for 31 percent of total assets. Bond funds account for another 35 percent, and equity funds make up the balance, 34 percent. Using the historical returns illustrated here and the distribution of mutual fund assets as a hypothetical investor's portfolio, I calculated that the "typical" mutual fund investor has the potential to return an average of 7.2 percent annually over the long run. That's only about 3 percent more each year than the rate of inflation and far below the return most investors expect.

With all the hype and hoopla that has accompanied the bull market in stocks and bonds recently, many investors have been led astray. Some have assumed very risky portfolios in an attempt to earn substantial returns that have very little chance of materializing. Others have assumed such conservative mixes of investments that their portfolios will produce little meaningful return. It's almost a sure bet that many investors' hopes and dreams will evaporate when portfolio returns fall far short of those they counted on to send their children to college or to retire comfortably.

Take these numbers to heart. Sit down and reevaluate your financial plan soon, if not today. Set realistic return expectations based on long-term historical averages. Adjust these hypothetical returns to reflect transactions costs, taxes and the rate of inflation. Finally, build and maintain a lifetime portfolio that will help you realize investment success—that is, ending up with enough money to achieve your goals.

It Pays To Keep Your Balance

Where should growth investors put their money these days? If you ponder the question of whether to invest in the stock market, you probably will find good reason to avoid equities, no matter what's going on in the financial markets. Frequently, investors so fear the stock market that they tend to underinvest in equity funds. However, history indicates that the best approach to equity investing is to spread capital across three categories of equities (large-cap, small-cap and international equity funds) and periodically rebalance that portfolio. That's because the relationship among the returns of blue chip stocks, small-cap stocks and international equities is less than perfect. In other words, when one asset category performs poorly, another category tends to perform much better. Equity investors who diversify across categories of equity mutual funds can lower the risk of their portfolios without sacrificing their return significantly. As a result, the risk per unit of return of a balanced portfolio of equities is minimized.

To illustrate what happens to a balanced portfolio of equities, I tracked the returns of blue chips, small caps and foreign stocks during the past two decades. (See Figure 11.2.) Here's what I found: If you are a conservative investor and wish to minimize total risk, the portfolio of choice is U.S. blue chip stocks. However, this portfolio, as you might expect, also delivers the lowest average annual return (13 percent, in this case). If your goal is to obtain the highest average annual rate of return (17.7 percent, in my study), U.S. small-cap stocks are your cup of tea. Of course, this portfolio is also the riskiest. If you want to obtain the greatest return while taking the least amount of risk, invest in the equally balanced portfolio. Note that its average return has been 2.4 percentage points greater than that of a blue chip equity portfolio, yet its standard deviation was only 0.80 percentage points greater. As a result, the balanced portfolio's risk per unit of return falls to 1.14.

Although many people want to invest where they believe they can earn the greatest short-run returns, prudent investors know that, by keeping their balances, they can keep their portfolios' returns from dropping radically because of a forecasting error (i.e., being in the wrong place at precisely the wrong time). In the case of equity fund investing, the appropriate strategy is to allocate capital across blue chip, small-cap and international equity funds.

FIGURE 11.2 □ A Balanced Approach to Growth Stock Investing

Year	Blue Chip Stocks	Small-Cap Stocks	International Stocks	Equal Allocation
1972	19.0%	4.4%	40.9%	21.4%
1973	−14.7	−30.9	−14.4	−19.9
1974	−26.5	−19.9	−24.0	−23.5
1975	37.2	52.8	37.5	42.5
1976	23.8	57.4	6.0	29.1
1977	−7.2	25.4	15.6	11.3
1978	6.6	23.5	34.3	21.5
1979	18.4	43.5	12.9	24.9
1980	32.4	39.9	25.1	32.5
1981	−4.9	13.9	−2.1	2.3
1982	21.4	28.8	−0.6	16.3
1983	22.5	39.7	25.1	29.1
1984	6.3	−6.7	5.1	1.6
1985	32.2	24.7	47.2	34.7
1986	18.5	6.9	55.5	26.9
1987	5.2	−9.3	5.0	0.3
1988	16.8	22.9	17.3	19.0
1989	31.5	10.0	23.9	21.8
1990	−3.2	−21.6	−12.0	−12.3
1991	30.5	44.6	11.1	28.7
1992	7.7	23.3	−14.0	15.6
Average Return	**13.0%**	**17.7%**	**14.4%**	**15.4%**
Standard Deviation	**16.7**	**24.4**	**21.0**	**17.5**
Risk/ Return	**1.29**	**1.38**	**1.49**	**1.14**

Lifetime Portfolio Management: A Primer

If you plan to retire (I know few people who don't), you'll need to save money now so you'll have income then. Over the long run, aggressive growth equity funds produce the highest total returns, but they are highly volatile and provide very little current income. Thus, they may not be well suited to all investors. However, for younger people who want to set aside dollars for their retirement, aggressive growth mutual funds are ideal investment vehicles because investors with long-range plans can tolerate a high degree of short-term price volatility.

When investing for retirement that will take place several decades in the future, your investment horizon should be long term. Thus, you can ignore week-to-week, month-to-month or even year-to-year variation in portfolio value. In fact, individuals who invest equal amounts of money regularly should welcome a high degree of portfolio volatility because their regular investments will buy a larger number of fund shares when share prices decline. Furthermore, because current dividend and interest income are subject to taxation when distributed, the needs of wealth-accumulating investors are better served by mutual funds that pay little or no current income. Thus, the full measure of return compounds over future years.

It is also no secret that bond funds provide the greatest current income. In addition, these funds generally hold a large number of different issues and thus protect you from the default risk you would face if you held a handful of bonds. Because retired individuals generally expect their investment portfolios to provide income, bond funds are highly touted to retirees by financial planners and other securities salespeople.

If investment life were that simple, you—as a wealth-accumulating investor—could merely invest in a few aggressive growth mutual funds, then exchange these funds for one or more bond funds when you retire. However, life is anything but simple. And neither is lifetime portfolio management.

Accumulating Wealth for Retirement

If you enjoy at least a five-year planning horizon, adopt a highly aggressive investment posture. Your goal should be to maximize investment return rather than minimize investment risk. Of course, risk management is important. As a wealth-accumulating investor, avoid taking unnecessary risks. You can do so by holding diversified portfolios and making regular cash contributions to your retirement programs. While all stocks fall during a bear market, a highly diversified portfolio of common stocks will eventually head for higher ground. And that cannot be said about a portfolio containing one or two stocks. Thus, by investing in a handful of growth and aggressive growth mutual funds, you guard against temporary losses turning into permanent ones. Furthermore, by investing equal dollar amounts at regular intervals, you benefit from dollar cost averaging. When stock prices are inordinately low, you accumulate more fund shares than you do when stock prices are inflated. Thus, when stock prices ultimately head higher, you magnify your investment returns. Finally, because you will not need your retirement contributions until the distant future, you have little need to hold cash reserves.

Keeping these points in mind, here is a simplified model portfolio for wealth-accumulating investors:

Wealth Accumulation

Aggressive Growth Funds	35%
Growth Funds	35
International Equity Funds	30

I recommend some diversification across types of capital appreciation funds because return relationships can be unstable over the short run. For example, during the past ten years, growth funds, on average, provided greater returns than aggressive growth funds, while aggressive growth funds provided greater returns over the past 15 to 20 years. I suggest investing in international equity funds because of the relatively low correlation of their returns with the returns of funds that invest solely in U.S. stocks. By combining international equities with domestic equities, you can reduce portfolio risk without sacrificing investment return. Furthermore, during periods marked by a weak dollar, these funds can produce handsome returns. During the past ten years, for instance, international equity funds returned an average of 17 percent compounded annually, or 2.5-plus percent more than the return of any other group of equity funds. Over the long run, this aggressive growth portfolio can be expected to return an average of between 11 and 14 percent annually.

Preretirement Portfolio

Retired investors generally require a balance between portfolio return and risk. First, because retirees usually do not contribute to their investment portfolios, they cannot temper losses by dollar cost averaging. Instead of adding to their investment portfolios, most retirees make regular withdrawals. Second, because these investors depend on income from their investments to support current consumption, they prefer predictable income streams. Finally, because of periodic withdrawals, retirees run the risk of having to sell fund shares when prices are depressed to meet their required monthly cash flow. The result is exactly opposite that of dollar cost averaging (i.e., retirees gain less on market rebounds because they must sell large numbers of securities when prices are depressed).

Investors who contemplate abruptly shifting from growth funds to income funds upon retirement also suffer from any temporary stock market declines that occur shortly before the shift occurs. For example, assume an aggressive growth portfolio is subject to a decline of 50 percent or more during steep bear stock markets. If such a bear market were to occur shortly before the portfolio holder retires, income could be permanently decreased by more than one-half. Thus, years of careful planning could be undone in a few short months.

To avoid this possibility, if you have less than five years until retirement, I recommend that you gradually reduce your portfolio risk. You can accomplish this by shifting from aggressive growth funds to growth and income funds and bond funds. One strategy follows:

Preretirement

Growth Funds	20%
Growth and Income Funds	20
International Equity Funds	15
Domestic Bond Funds	15

International Bond Funds	15
Money Market Funds	15

Note that more than one-half of this portfolio is invested in equity funds. Thus, the portfolio has the potential to provide capital growth as well as income. The 45 percent allocation to bond funds and money market funds provides stability as well as current income. As a result, you could expect this portfolio to decline by one-third less than an aggressive portfolio during a steep bear market. However, over a five-year market cycle, the sample portfolio should return about 9 to 10 percent annually. Thus, only a 20 percent reduction in long-term total return accompanies a 40 percent reduction in investment risk.

A Growth and Income Retirement Portfolio

As a new retiree, you should remember that your investment portfolio must support you for 20 years or more. In other words, if you have recently retired, you should still invest for the long term. That means you must continue to seek some growth of investment capital to offset the impact of inflation. For example, if consumer prices rise at their historical average of 3 percent annually, the prices of goods and services would be 80 percent higher 20 years from now. Thus, even a modest amount of inflation can devastate a retiree.

Consider the plight of a retired investor who purchased "safe" government bonds with 20-year maturities a couple of decades ago. If this investor had invested $200,000 in these bonds in 1970, the portfolio (then yielding 7.75 percent) would have provided an annual income of $15,000. Twenty years later, this portfolio would still provide $15,000 in annual income. However, because of escalating consumer prices, it would have taken an annual income of $50,000 to maintain the same standard of living the investor enjoyed when he made the initial investment. Or, to put it another way, the purchasing power of a $15,000 annual income stream would have fallen to $4,500 by the time the 20-year bonds matured, and the purchasing power of the initial $200,000 bond investment would have fallen to $60,000!

To protect your investment income and portfolio value from the detrimental effects of inflation, design an investment portfolio to provide some growth in income and capital over the long term. This, of course, means investing in equities. Following is a model portfolio that provides both growth and a high level of current income:

Retirement: Growth and Income

Growth Funds	10%
Growth and Income Funds	10
International Equity Funds	10
Domestic Bond Funds	30
International Bond Funds	20
Money Market Funds	20

Note that this portfolio contains a 30 percent allocation to equity funds. These funds, in addition to providing some current income, can be expected to grow by an average of about 7 percent annually and thus to provide an overall portfolio growth rate of approximately 2 percent each year (about two-thirds of the inflation rate during the past 50 years). Furthermore, during periods when stock prices advance at a greater-than-average pace, an investor can rebalance the portfolio by selling some equity shares and diverting the proceeds to bond and money market funds. By taking profits when stock prices are inordinately high, the investor obtains the potential to increase the portfolio's average growth rate. Furthermore, this portfolio can provide a greater current income than the investor can generally obtain from bank CDs, T-bills or money market mutual funds. Finally, because of the large allocation to fixed-income investments, the portfolio possesses less than one-third of the risk of the stock market.

Portfolios for Highly Conservative Retirees

It may come as a bit of a surprise to some investors that my recommended portfolio for very conservative retirees does not differ much from the portfolio I recommended for younger retirees. In fact, my allocations are exactly the same: 30 percent to equity funds, 50 percent to bond funds and 20 percent to money market funds. The only difference is that I recommend that you shift the 10 percent growth fund allocation to growth and income funds (bringing the total allocation to this fund category to 20 percent). This shift will both decrease portfolio variability (risk) and increase current income. Generally, growth and income funds have betas less than 0.50 and provide about 200 basis points less yield than T-bills. This reduces the downside risk to less than one-fourth that of the stock market and provides a growth potential of more than 1.5 percent annually.

Retirement: Conservative

Growth and Income Funds	20%
International Equity Funds	10
Domestic Bond Funds	30
International Bond Funds	20
Money Market Funds	20

Although I have attempted to provide a bare-bones outline of portfolio strategies for broad groups of investors with varying income and capital appreciation needs, you can see that maintaining a lifetime investment plan can be somewhat complex. However, the proliferation of mutual funds has simplified your ability to implement lifetime financial planning. As an individual investor, you can obtain a high degree of diversification by investing in mutual funds that specialize in particular categories of financial assets. Thus, you can control investment risk to a much greater extent today than you could only a few years ago. In addition, because each mutual fund's portfolio manager selects individual stocks and bonds, you can concentrate your decision making to allocation decisions and individual mutual fund selections rather than choosing specific stocks and bonds.

An All-Weather Mutual Fund Portfolio

The largest benefit of mutual fund investing is the risk reduction that results from portfolio diversification. By investing in a diversified equity fund, for example, rather than in one or two common stocks, you reduce your investment risk by roughly two-thirds without sacrificing any long-run return. Investing in a bond fund rather than in a single bond limits capital losses that could result from default.

SMART STRATEGIES *An all-weather portfolio provides the best of two worlds—greater returns and less risk—for the risk-conscious growth investor.*

While most investors generally understand the concept of not putting all your eggs in one basket, which baskets do you use, and how many eggs do you place in each?

To obtain total portfolio diversification, at least in theory, purchase the "market" portfolio. This portfolio consists of all types of assets combined in the proportions in which they exist throughout the world. That is, the truly diversified portfolio contains a little bit of everything. Because this portfolio is impossible to construct, a truly diversified portfolio exists only in theory. However, you can greatly reduce investment risk by diversifying across a broad class of assets (i.e., by moving closer to the market portfolio described in investment theory). Your portfolio should contain stocks, bonds, cash, precious metals and real estate.

The object of such diversification, of course, is to iron out the widespread fluctuation in investment wealth that can occur when only a single asset or class of assets is held. For example, the conditions that generally cause stock prices to fall (e.g., rising commodity prices and interest rates) generally cause the price of gold to rise. Thus, a decline in the value of one segment of the portfolio offsets an increase in the value of another segment. Furthermore, a well-diversified portfolio transcends political and geographical boundaries. Thus, include worldwide rather than country-specific assets in your portfolio. Although the various economies of the world are becoming more interdependent and therefore tend to expand and contract in concert, very often such movements occur with varying time lags. When one economy contracts, another may continue to expand for a while longer. In addition, global portfolios contain less risk than locally concentrated portfolios because foreign exchange risk is reduced. That is, as currency values fluctuate, gains in the value of one currency offset relative declines in another.

Several years ago, I developed a highly diversified portfolio that I manage for conservative, yet growth-oriented clients. I call it an "all-weather" portfolio. It consists of mutual funds that concentrate their investments in eight categories of financial assets. While far from a perfect substitute for the theoretical market portfolio, my All-Weather Portfolio has produced double-digit returns while exposing my clients to about one-half the volatility of the stock market. The eight categories of assets the portfolio contains include the following:

1. U.S. Stocks—Large Companies
2. U.S. Stocks—Small Companies
3. International Stocks
4. U.S. Bonds
5. International Bonds
6. Precious Metals
7. Real Estate
8. Money Market Assets

I have chosen to exclude an investment in real estate in this portfolio for a number of reasons. First, very few mutual funds invest directly in real estate, and those that do tend to be organized as limited partnerships and thus possess limited liquidity. Second, the portfolios of most investors tend to contain large percentages of real estate—usually their personal residences. Third, many corporations have vast real estate holdings, which affect common stock values. Thus, by investing in common stocks, you invest in real estate indirectly.

A simplistic approach to managing the all-weather portfolio would be to spread your investment capital equally across all seven asset classes (i.e., allocate about 14 percent of your investment capital to each asset class). While this method is not scientific, such an allocation is relatively close to the ideal. I chose a slightly different tack. I obtained estimates of world wealth by asset class. I then excluded real estate, recomputed the percentage of world wealth in each remaining asset class and set my allocation targets to the nearest multiple of 5 percent. Thus, the long-run allocation targets for the all-weather portfolio are as follows:

Small-Cap Equity Funds	15%
Large-Cap Equity Funds	15
International Equity Funds	15
U.S. Bond Funds	20
International Bond Funds	10
Gold Funds	10
Money Market Funds	15

You can take two approaches when managing your own all-weather portfolio: passive or active. The *passive approach* holds that, because the goal of an all-weather portfolio is risk reduction, gains in the value of one segment of the portfolio will largely offset declines in another. If you knew which asset class would produce the greatest returns during the year, you could allocate all your capital to that asset class. However, by managing the portfolio in this way, you increase risk due to forecasting errors, which the all-weather portfolio was designed to limit in the first place.

The *active approach* is based on the notion that some degree of active management can benefit your portfolio as long as reallocations among asset classes are modest and are not made frequently. Thus, when it appears that one segment of the portfolio contains assets that are highly overvalued, reduce the proportion of capital committed to that segment. By reallocating in this manner, you may increase long-run returns without having to forecast the short-run direction of asset prices (for relative values rather than trends are used as the basis for reallocating capital).

I have opted for a variation of the active approach, which I call a *semi-active approach.* Figure 11.3 shows the allocation boundaries for each asset class. Note that these boundaries require a minimum of 5 percent allocation to each investment category, no matter how unattractive its return potential may appear. On the other hand, I have set a maximum 20 percent allocation to each category. My discipline requires that I allocate no more than 20 percent of port-

FIGURE 11.3 □ Asset Allocation Boundaries

Asset Class	Allocation Range	Current Allocation
Small-Cap Equity Funds	10–20%	15%
Large-Cap Equity Funds	10–20	10
International Equity Funds	10–20	10
U.S. Bond Funds	10–30	30
International Bond Funds	5–15	10
Gold Funds	5–15	5
Money Market Funds	5–25	20

folio assets to any category, no matter how optimistic I may be about that category's return prospects.

Figure 11.4 compares the returns of the all-weather portfolio (using an equal allocation strategy and rebalancing the portfolio at the end of each calendar year) with returns from T-bills and common stocks (the total return of the S&P 500 index). Over the entire 1973 to 1993 period, investment in T-bills (a riskless asset) provided a 7.3 percent compound annual return, or 1.5 percent more than the rate of inflation. An average-risk common stock portfolio returned 11.3 percent annually, or 5.7 percent more than the rate of change in the Consumer Price Index. The all-weather portfolio provided the greatest long-run return: 12.2 percent each year, or 6.6 percent more than the rate of inflation. And it did so while providing only minimal risk exposure. Note that the all-weather portfolio lost ground during just two years (1974 and 1990) versus five years for the stock market. Furthermore, while the common stock portfolio declined by as much as 26.5 percent during one year, the maximum decline in the all-weather portfolio was 3.7 percent. Finally, note that during the 1973 to 1974 bear market, common stock plunged 37.3 percent, while the all-weather portfolio declined in value by slightly more than 1 percent.

When viewed over a 20-year period 1973 to 1993, the all-weather portfolio appears to provide the best of two worlds—greater investment returns and reduced investment risk. Although

FIGURE 11.4 □ Investment Returns, 1973–1993

Year	T-Bills	S&P Index	All-Weather Portfolio
1973	6.9	–14.7	2.8
1974	8.0	–26.5	1.3
1975	5.8	37.2	21.9
1976	5.1	23.8	14.2
1977	5.1	–7.2	11.9
1978	7.2	6.6	17.3
1979	10.4	18.4	20.4
1980	11.2	32.4	28.6
1981	14.7	–4.9	–1.9
1982	10.5	21.4	17.8
1983	8.8	22.5	12.1
1984	9.8	6.3	2.2
1985	7.7	32.2	24.8
1986	6.2	18.5	23.7
1987	5.5	5.2	8.9
1988	6.4	16.8	10.3
1989	8.4	31.5	11.3
1990	7.8	–3.1	–3.7
1991	5.6	30.6	17.4
1992	3.5	7.7	4.2
1993	3.0	10.0	17.5
Compound Return	7.3%	11.3%	12.2%
Value of $10,000	$43,900	$94,700	$112,100

the least risky posture is investment in T-bills, their return barely tops the rate of inflation. A $10,000 T-bill investment made at the beginning of 1970 would have grown to $43,900 by the end of 1993. On the other hand, a similar investment made in the all-weather portfolio would have grown to $112,100 while exposing investors to a maximum annual decline of less than 2 percent.

During the stock market's meltdown of October 1987, when stock prices plunged by nearly 30 percent, the all-weather portfolio declined by slightly more than 7 percent. And that loss was largely erased two months later. Thus, risk-conscious, growth-oriented investors should seriously consider adopting an all-weather portfolio management approach. Although the return from this portfolio may roughly match the stock market's return over the long run, its risk is less than one-half that of the typical equity mutual fund.

12

It's a Family Affair

One of the interesting developments in the evolution of the mutual fund industry has been the creation of the multi-fund mutual fund family. These "families" sponsor numerous funds, act as the funds' distributors, serve as the funds' investment advisers and assume the administrative responsibilities for operating the funds. Some fund families, such as Fidelity, provide sales, advisory and support services for more than 100 mutual funds. Others, such as T. Rowe Price, offer special services like personal computer access to shareholder account data.

The growth of the family concept was no doubt fostered by the creation of the telephone switch privilege, which allows you to switch your investments from one fund to another in the same family by telephoning toll free a family's service center. In most instances, these switches are made within 24 hours of request and are free of charge.

Investing in the funds offered by a single fund family provides several benefits. First, you receive a single statement listing all of your fund holdings and recent transactions. This reduces the pile of paper you can accumulate when investing in several funds drawn from numerous fund families. Also, it is very easy to change the composition of your investment portfolio or to liquidate fund holdings by making a single telephone call. Finally, by concentrating your investments in a single family, you eliminate the downtime that occurs when you liquidate your investment in one fund from a particular family and subsequently invest in a fund from another family. The downtime results from the time it takes to receive in the mail a check from one fund, then mail a second check and a purchase application to another fund residing in a different family. Checks that spend several days or weeks in the mail or a fund's processing department while the stock and bond markets march onward can reduce significantly a portfolio's returns over your investment lifetime.

Although the concept of confining all of your mutual fund investments to one fund family may seem appealing, this strategy has its drawbacks. First, no fund family corners the market on funds with the best performance potential. Confining your investments to a single family could therefore reduce your portfolio's performance over the long run. In addition, chances are no fund family offers all of the funds that might serve your investment needs. When you confine your investments to a single fund family, your portfolio may not completely fulfill your investment needs or objectives. Finally, the expansion of mutual fund services at major discount brokerage firms now allows you to assemble a portfolio consisting of numerous funds drawn from many fund families. At the same time, these services provide both the opportunity to switch among the funds with a single telephone call and the convenience of a single monthly account statement.

The following list describes 25 major mutual fund families. I have included telephone numbers so that you may contact a fund family and obtain literature that describes its offerings and special services.

Major Mutual Fund Families

Alliance Capital Management
500 Plaza Dr., Secaucus, NJ 07094 Telephone: 800-221-5672

This fund family offers mostly load funds. Various classes of shares allow you to select how you will pay sales charges. A and B class shares are either front-end or back-end loaded, and C class shares are sold with a level 12b-1 fee in lieu of either a front-end or back-end load. In mid-1993, the family acquired Equitable's mutual fund family of funds.

American Capital
P.O. Box 3528, Houston, TX 77253 Telephone: 800-421-5666

American Capital is one of the nation's oldest mutual fund families. Its funds are sold to the public with relatively steep sales commissions. However, the family boasts some of the best performing funds in the industry. A number of its funds are managed by a team of managers rather than by a single "star" manager.

Babson
2440 Pershing Rd.,
3 Crown Center,
Kansas City, MO 64108 Telephone: 800-422-2766

The Babson funds are 100 percent no-load funds. While the family offers both taxable and tax-exempt bond funds, its expertise lies in the management of equity portfolios, especially portfolios consisting of small-cap stocks. Since its inception in 1983, Babson Enterprise has chalked up one of the best performance records of all small-cap funds. Unfortunately, this fund is now closed to new investors. However, its small-cap index fund is also directed by Peter Schlieman of Babson Enterprise fame. Large-cap investors may wish to check out its value fund offering.

Benham Group
1665 Charleston Rd., Mountain View,
CA 94043 Telephone: 800-472-3389

Long noted for its offering of well-managed fixed-income funds, this family added a precious metals fund (Benham Gold Equities Index) in 1992 and its first equity fund (Benham Utility Income) in 1993. Long an innovator, Benham introduced the first government-only money market fund and was the first to offer target maturity zero-coupon bond funds. All of its funds are sold directly to the public without sales charges of any kind.

Capital Research & Management
333 S. Hope St., 52nd Floor,
Los Angeles, CA 90071 Telephone: 800-421-9900

This well-marketed fund family consists of more than two dozen funds with more than $90 billion in total assets and more than 4 million shareholder accounts. The family's flagship fund, Investment Company of America, has been a steady and consistent performer for much of its 60-year existence. Its funds are conservatively managed with a value bent. The company's strength lies in its large research department spread around the globe. Rather than a "star" management concept, this fund family uses a multidimensional approach under which a fund is divided into several segments, with an independent portfolio manager assigned to each segment.

Columbia
1301 S. W. 5th Ave., P.O. Box 1350,
Portland, OR 97207 Telephone: 800-547-1707

This Oregon-based company was created in 1967 when it launched its first mutual fund, the Columbia Growth Fund. Today, the company, which is employee owned, manages nearly $15 billion in mutual fund assets, commingled trusts and private accounts. Columbia is most noted for its equity fund management. Its funds, sold without sales charges, are managed with a team approach and a top-down investment style.

Dodge & Cox
1 Sansome, San Francisco, CA 94104 Telephone: 415-434-0311

Although this small family offers only three funds, all have been solid performers. For more than a half-century, Dodge & Cox has invested in established companies that possess the potential to deliver long-term growth of earnings, but are out of favor with investors. The firm hides no secret to its successful mutual fund performance record. A decided value bent and wide portfolio diversification have rewarded the family's shareholders for decades.

Evergreen Funds
2500 Westchester Ave.,
Purchase, NY 10577 Telephone: 800-235-0064

First Union Corp. purchased this family of no-load funds in late 1993. The combined firm now holds more than $7 billion in assets, and more than two dozen funds are marketed through First Union branch banks. The company is well known for its expertise in the small-cap sector of the stock market. Its most popular fund, the Evergreen Fund, was organized in 1972.

Fidelity Investments

82 Devonshire St., Boston, MA 02109 Telephone: 800-544-8888

This family of funds has been the most active player in the mutual fund industry. It has more funds, shareholder accounts and money under management in its funds than any other family. Best known for its aggressive marketing, Fidelity manages some of the best equity funds in the business. At the hub is the 50-year-old Magellan Fund, whose assets now top $30 billion. The company is also known for its innovative management, which in recent years popularized the sector fund concept with its Select Portfolios, began quoting some fund prices each hour, launched a discount brokerage firm and added "storefront" sales offices in major cities. Although most of Fidelity's funds are sold with low front-end loads and modest redemption fees, all investors should find something they like in this 100-plus-fund family.

Founders

2930 E. 3rd Ave., Denver, CO 80206 Telephone: 800-525-2440

Founders, which has been an investment adviser since the late 1930s, is another example of a small, yet well-run fund family. Its $2 billion in assets are spread among nine funds. Its equity funds—the most popular being the Frontier and Discovery Funds—have a decided small-cap flavor. In managing each fund, Founders combines a team approach with a lead portfolio manager. The former is responsible for developing a list of preferred investments, while the latter makes individual selections and runs the fund on a day-to-day basis.

Franklin/Templeton Funds

777 Mariners Island Blvd.,
San Mateo, CA 94403 Telephone: 800-342-5236

Franklin Resources is a publicly traded financial services company that provides primarily advisory, distribution and administrative services for the Franklin Group of Funds. In business since 1947, the Franklin

Group is best known for its fixed-income funds, especially municipal bond funds. Franklin obtained extensive international equity fund exposure when it acquired Templeton Funds in 1992. The Templeton Funds organization retained its autonomy in advising and servicing the Franklin/Templeton Funds. Most funds in this family are sold with front-end loads which are also levied on the reinvestment of dividends.

IAI Group

3700 First Bank Place, P.O. Box 357,
Minneapolis, MN 55440 Telephone: 800-945-3863

IAI, which began operating as an investment adviser in 1947, manages more than $12 billion for institutional and individual investors. The company entered the mutual fund business in 1971 when it launched the IAI Stock Fund (renamed the IAI Growth & Income Fund). Now a subsidiary of the London-based Hill Samuel Group, the company offers both domestic and international equity funds. Equity selections are based on fundamental analysis that stresses investment in quality companies and the practice of risk management.

INVESCO Funds Group

P.O. Box 2040, Denver, CO 80217 Telephone: 800-525-8085

Originally founded in 1932 as the Investors Independent Corporation, the company marketed its first fund in 1935. It adopted a no-load format in 1972, was purchased by Britannia Arrow in 1984 and changed its name from Financial Programs to INVESCO in 1991. The company is best known for its long-established conservative equity funds. Recently, INVESCO began an aggressive marketing program and has added several new funds, especially in the international equity area.

Janus Group

100 Fillmore St., Suite 300,
Denver, CO 80206 Telephone: 800- 525-3713

Founded in 1970, the family now consists of a wide array of funds. It is probably best known for the James Craig-managed Janus Fund, which has nearly $10 billion in assets. Over the years, its domestic equity funds have achieved enviable performance records by riding bull markets and heading for the safety of cash during stormy markets. This is a feat few other fund families have been able to duplicate. In recent years, some of the Janus Group's popular funds have been forced to close their doors to new shareholders.

Mutual Series Funds

51 JFK Pkwy., Short Hills, NJ 07078 Telephone: 800-448-3863

Founded by Max Heine, the firm's adviser, Heine Securities was acquired by Michael Price after Heine's death. Price, who serves as the portfolio manager of each of its four funds, has built an enviable reputation as a "bottom fisherman," who finds and capitalizes on hidden values in troubled companies. Unfortunately, the family's most successful funds, Mutual Shares, Mutual Qualified and Mutual Discovery, have recently closed their doors to new shareholders.

Neuberger & Berman

605 3rd Ave., 2nd Floor,
New York, NY 10158 Telephone: 800-877-9700

This fund adviser is noted for its consistent, conservative and value-based asset selection style. Its oldest and most popular fund has posted a double-digit average annual return during its 45-year history. All of the company's funds are no-load funds that possess modest management fees and low expense ratios. Recently, the company has begun to aggressively market its funds, which have been excellent vehicles for conservative, growth-oriented investors.

Nicholas Funds

700 N. Water St., Suite 1010,
Milwaukee, WI 53202 Telephone: 414-272-6133

Founded by Albert ("Ab") O. Nicholas in the late 1960s, the family offers a half-dozen funds, including its flagship fund, the $3 billion Nicholas Fund. Operating with a 100 percent no-load format, a long-term investment horizon and modest expenses, the firm's funds have achieved better-than-average long-term performance records. Although he did not start out this way, Ab Nicholas is an avowed value investor who generally pays a price-earnings multiple no higher than a company's long-term annual growth rate when selecting stocks for his equity fund portfolios. Once selected, a stock tends to stay in a Nicholas Funds portfolio for an average of three to five years. Unfortunately, the well-managed Nicholas II and Limited Edition funds are closed to new investors.

Nuveen
333 W. Wacker Dr., Chicago, IL 60606 Telephone: 800-351-4100

This fund manager specializes solely in tax-free funds and unit investment trusts. It began operations shortly before the turn of the century as a distributor of municipal bonds and an adviser to municipal bond issuers. Recently, the company initiated a public stock offering, and its shares are now traded on the New York Stock Exchange. Its funds, which carry a 4.75 percent front-end sales charge, are marketed exclusively by brokerage firms and other financial institutions.

SAFECO
P.O. Box 34890, Seattle, WA 98124 Telephone: 800-624-5711

The company began operations in the early 1920s solely as an insurance company serving the northwestern part of the United States. SAFECO founded its mutual fund subsidiary in 1967. The subsidiary is unique in that it is one of the few insurance-company-owned funds with a no-load format. Its funds currently have about $2 billion in total assets. The company's equity funds tend to follow an out-of-favor, value-based investment selection philosophy. Thus, it's no accident that SAFECO's funds have well served the needs of conservative investors. The family expects to increase significantly its number of fund offerings in the next couple of years.

Scudder
160 Federal St., 12th Floor,
Boston, MA 02100 Telephone: 800-225-2470

Scudder, Stevens Clark, a highly diversified financial services firm, was founded in 1913. Its $70 billion under management is almost equally split between its mutual funds and its private account management business. Scudder created the first no-load mutual fund in the United States in 1928. It created the first global equity fund in 1953. All of its open-end funds now operate as pure no-load funds. In addition to operating its own funds under the Scudder banner, the company also serves as the investment adviser to the AARP fund family.

SteinRoe
P.O. Box 1162, Chicago, IL 60690 Telephone: 800-338-2550

The firm was founded in 1932 to manage private accounts for individual investors. It offered its first mutual fund in 1949. All of SteinRoe's funds are pure no-load funds, which possess no sales charges of any kind. Although the company's mutual funds are well managed, it has never been known as an aggressive marketer. As a result, SteinRoe has not experienced the growth of other large fund families. The company was acquired by Liberty Financial, a subsidiary of Liberty Mutual, in 1986. In recent years, it has trimmed the number of funds it offers.

Strong Funds
100 Heritage Reserve,
Menomonee Falls, WI 53201 Telephone: 800-368-3863

The company's cofounder, Dick Strong, learned the portfolio management business while working at a small Wisconsin bank with Albert Nicholas. Both he and Nicholas left the bank to manage a mutual fund in the late 1960s, and Strong later teamed with Bill Corneliuson (who recently retired) to establish the Strong Funds in 1981. The family's funds, long noted for seeking a combination of income and capital appreciation, are actively managed and may move swiftly into cash or bonds if the stock market turns stormy. As a consequence, a number of its funds have been strong performers during both bull and bear stock markets.

T. Rowe Price
100 E. Pratt St., Baltimore, MD 21202 Telephone: 800-638-5660

The T. Rowe Price fund company is the successor to the investment counseling business founded by the legendary Thomas Rowe in the late 1930s. The company, whose stock is not publicly traded, is best known for serving the needs of company-sponsored profit- sharing and defined-contribution retirement plans. In addition to well-managed funds, the company is also noted for its high level of customer service. Its investment-oriented publications are educational and informative. Recently, the company initiated a new service that allows fund shareholders to access their account information using personal computers. All of its funds are 100 percent no-load.

Twentieth Century
4500 Main St., P.O. Box 418210,
Kansas City, MO 64111 Telephone: 800-345-2021

Founded by James Stowers in the late 1950s, the company enjoyed the bulk of its growth in assets during the early 1990s. In managing its equity portfolios, the company uses an earnings- momentum-driven computer screen to locate promising investments. Individual selections must then pass the scrutiny of a portfolio management team. Twentieth Century's equity funds possess some of the highest betas in the industry and thus are highly volatile. In addition, the adviser's philosophy requires it to maintain fully invested positions in bad markets as well as good. Although risky, its equity funds possess the best 20-year performance track records in the industry.

United Funds
6300 Lamar Ave., P.O. Box 29217,
Shawnee Mission, KS 66201 Telephone: 913-236-2000

Kansas-based Waddell & Reed guide the conservatively managed funds in this family. Although highly sensitive to its shareholders' needs, the company sets a relatively high 5.75 percent front-end sales charge on each of its funds. It has not joined the mutual fund industry's stampede to add a large number of new funds or balloon the assets under management.

Vanguard Group
Vanguard Financial Center,
Valley Forge, PA 19482 Telephone: 800-635-1511

Under the direction of John Bogle, this fund family has established a reputation for providing the lowest cost funds in the mutual fund industry. All funds are sold without sales charges and possess modest expense ratios. The company has been able to control fund expenses because of its unique organization structure whereby the funds own Vanguard's administrative subsidiary and provide services at cost. Management fees are also very modest. In addition, many of the family's funds operate under an index format and thus lack both portfolio managers and management fees. The company has attracted an enviable following among investors and controls more than $120 billion in assets, which are spread across more than 4 million shareholder accounts.

13

One-Stop Shopping

As I have described it, investing in mutual funds is not difficult. You find a fund in which you would like to invest, call the fund to ask for a prospectus and purchase application, fill out the application and send it with your check to the fund's distributor. The fund's custodian bank holds your shares and sends you periodic statements detailing the progress of your investment. Although you can switch your investment in one fund to another in the same fund family by making a phone call, you must repeat the whole process when you want to exchange an investment in one fund for another offered by a different family. In other words, you must request in writing that shares of the former fund be redeemed, wait for the fund to send you a check, deposit the check in your bank account, then send a personal check to the distributor of the fund you wish to buy. If you repeat these activities for a dozen or more funds, the process can take time. Not only do you end up swimming in account statements every month, you can spend several weeks each year out of the market while waiting for redemption checks or sending checks to newly selected funds.

Several discount brokers now offer an alternative to the mass of paperwork that accompanies investing with several different fund families. Charles Schwab's Tom Taggart puts it simply: "Not all top-rated funds are in the same fund family." Schwab's Mutual Fund Marketplace, Fidelity Investments' FundsNetwork and Jack White & Company's Mutual Fund Network each offers you the opportunity to invest in hundreds of load and no-load funds from several fund families in one-stop shopping. For a small commission charge, these discount brokers will buy and sell fund shares for you. The brokerage firm keeps the shares, and you receive a consolidated statement of your fund holdings every month. Furthermore, many discount brokers have begun to offer no-brokerage-commission trading in mutual funds. The funds that participate in these no-transaction-fee (NTF) programs reimburse the brokers for selling the fund's shares by allocating a portion of the funds' brokerage commissions to the discounters. Thus, you enjoy the convenience of being able to switch among mutual fund families with a single telephone call. You eliminate investment downtime, and you pay relatively low fees (or no additional fees) to conduct business. Though the differences among the three brokers outlined below may appear insignificant, depending on the amount of capital you invest, the amount of trading you do and your general investment style, one of the firms may better suit you than the others.

SMART STRATEGIES *Discount brokers now offer an alternative to the mass of paperwork and investment downtime that accompanies investing with several different fund families. One-stop shopping can save you time and money.*

Charles Schwab's Mutual Fund Marketplace (800-266-5623) offers about 700 mutual funds from which to choose. Of these, Schwab's OneSource program includes about 200 funds from 25 no-load families, which are available to investors on an NTF basis. What's in it for Schwab? you may ask. The no-load fund groups with which Schwab contracts pay Schwab a nominal fee for attracting the assets to their families of funds. Because Schwab essentially maintains the accounts—fielding investors' telephone calls, sending prospectuses, assembling statements and so on—a fund group earns hassle-free assets through the OneSource program and does not necessarily mind handing over a small portion of its income. Investors find the program ultraconvenient because they need remember only one telephone number—Schwab's—and they receive one statement that details investment activity. Investors also may purchase load funds through the Marketplace, in which case, they are required to pay loads as they apply to individual funds. The advantage ends when you purchase a no-load fund through Schwab that does not participate in the OneSource program. For this type of purchase, you pay Schwab a transaction fee according to a fee schedule. Therefore, it is to your advantage to purchase the fund directly from the sponsor. The OneSource division of Schwab's Mutual Fund Marketplace has become so popular among no-load investors that assets have swelled beyond $7 billion since it began operations a few years ago.

Fidelity Investors' FundsNetwork program (800-544-9697) is set up similarly to Schwab's Mutual Fund Marketplace and flaunts the same major advantage: the ability to purchase several no-load mutual funds from among different families without paying transaction fees. Fidelity profits the same way Schwab does from its relationship with no-load groups, and you experience a similar degree of convenience (one statement, one telephone call, etc.). Although Fidelity offers significantly more funds to choose from overall (about 1,700), only about 100 of these are sold NTF (not including Fidelity funds). Additionally, if you purchase a no-load fund not offered through Fidelity's NTF program, your transaction fee is higher at Fidelity than at Schwab (sometimes significantly, depending on the investment amount).

You will find one advantage to Fidelity's FundsNetwork that you will not at another discount broker—the availability of Fidelity funds on an NTF basis. The Fidelity funds have quite a following, and fans of this group may choose not only from among several no-load groups, but also from among several Fidelity offerings, all on an NTF basis.

Although other discount brokers probably would love to get their hands on Fidelity's high-quality no-load funds for their NTF programs, the chances of Fidelity allowing this are slim. If you plan to invest primarily in Fidelity's funds, with few no-load exceptions, this program should be right for you.

Jack White & Company (800-233-3411) offers more funds in its NTF Mutual Fund Network (254) than Schwab (about 200), and its list of available funds differs significantly from Schwab's. Additionally, its transaction fee for the purchase or sale of nonparticipating no-load funds is less than Schwab's. However, each buy or sell transaction has a $5,000 minimum. Neither Schwab nor Fidelity imposes minimum dollar amounts on transactions. Jack White saddles transactions of less than $5,000 with a $27 fee.

If you plan to trade in large chunks, though, consider Jack White. This broker provides the same conveniences as the others and offers more funds and lower fees. Additionally, Jack White sets no limit on the number of short-term transactions, while both Schwab and Fidelity limit investors to five short-term trades each year.

Funds of Funds

A growing number of mutual fund families also have begun to offer one-stop shopping services. These fund families have created mutual funds that invest in several other funds in the same families. These "funds of funds" do not levy additional advisory fees or saddle investors with additional operating expenses. Thus, you obtain a managed portfolio of mutual funds while assuming only a pro rata share of the expenses of the funds in that portfolio.

The Vanguard Star Fund, for example, invests in nine other mutual funds offered by Vanguard: Vanguard Windsor, Windsor II, U.S. Growth Portfolio, Morgan Growth, PRIMECAP, Explorer, GNMA Portfolio, Long-Term Corporate Bond Portfolio and Money Market Reserves. And how much money must you invest to achieve such a high level of diversification? A mere $500, which is considerably less than the $3,000 minimum initial investment required by other Vanguard funds.

T. Rowe Price offers two fund of funds alternatives. The Spectrum Growth Fund, which invests in T. Rowe Price's International Stock, Growth Stock, New Horizons, New Era, Growth & Income, Equity Income and Prime Reserve funds, provides a highly diversified equity fund portfolio. The Spectrum Income Fund invests in a variety of income funds, including T. Rowe Price's High Yield, New Income, International Bond, Equity Income, GNMA, Short-Term Bond and Prime Reserve funds. The income fund's modest allocation to the Equity Income Fund provides a slight hedge against inflation.

All three of these funds—the Vanguard Star Fund and T. Rowe Price's Spectrum Growth and Spectrum Income funds—are perfect for those with little money to spread across a number of individual mutual funds (for example, a young couple with a few thousand dollars set aside, a child with a small college savings fund or anyone just beginning to save and invest). In fact, these funds are ideal for those new to the game who don't have the knowledge to begin assembling portfolios of mutual funds or the time to constantly monitor these portfolios.

Beware of the Drawbacks

Although investing this way offers a great deal of appeal, you need to be aware of a few drawbacks. First, not all funds in the same fund family boast the same quality. In fact, it's highly improbable that all of the funds in a single family possess top performance potential. Thus, performance in such a portfolio may be a bit more disappointing than performance in a portfolio of funds drawn from several different fund families. It's also probable that some components of a fund of funds portfolio won't fit your investment goals exactly. However, the fund of funds approach is an excellent way to begin investing in mutual funds. As you gain knowledge and experience, you can shift your capital from these funds to a mutual fund portfolio you assemble and manage yourself.

14

Getting Off on the Right Foot: A Mutual Fund Shopping List

In the previous chapters of this book, I have shown you various mutual fund selection and portfolio management strategies to help you become a better mutual fund investor. Although no guarantee of investment success exists, if you practice these smart strategies, you will shift the investment odds in your favor. Like the house's edge in gaming casinos, individuals who tilt the investment odds in their favor and stay in the game over the long term can expect to earn higher returns than they otherwise could.

At present, more than 6,000 mutual funds are available to investors. During 1994 alone, more than 2,400 funds either began selling shares or were in the process of registering with the SEC. The proliferation of mutual funds during the last couple of decades has benefited investors greatly. Investment opportunities never before available to individuals now pack their plates. Think of any investment style and asset selection strategy, and chances are you can find at least a handful of funds that meet these criteria. With a greater freedom of choice, any investor should be able to build a portfolio of mutual funds that meets the investor's needs and objectives while staying well within his or her risk tolerance zone.

Although the astronomical expansion in the number and types of funds has been a boon to individual investors, it has also confounded the fund selection process for many novice investors. With so many funds available, new investors virtually drown in the flood of funds offered. If you are one of these investors, this chapter should provide some assistance.

100 Smart Ways To Start Your Shopping

The following list of 100 equity funds was drawn from five fund categories: aggressive growth, growth, growth and income, international and precious metals. These funds are not necessarily the best funds currently available, although all possess the characteristics of funds with better-than-average performance potential. In fact, at one time or another, many of these funds have ranked among the performance leaders when compared to their peers. For the novice investor, this list of 100 equity funds is an excellent place to begin the hunt for suitable mutual fund investments. Even experienced investors may find a gem or two that they have not previously considered. Thus, this list of equity funds should benefit most investors.

SMART STRATEGIES *Begin your investment program today. You will never be a successful investor if you never invest!*

You will find a brief description of each fund's investment style and asset selection strategy, along with an outline of sales charges (if any) and the fund's toll-free telephone number. If any of the funds on this list piques your interest, call the fund to request a prospectus, the latest shareholders' report and a purchase application. Study these documents carefully, and use the techniques you have seen in previous chapters. Most important of all, begin your investment program today. Remember, you will never be a successful investor if you never invest. Reduce the costs of investing, maintain a highly diversified portfolio, invest for the long term, add capital to your portfolio whenever you can and keep your portfolio within your risk tolerance zone. Now you have the requirements for investment success. Follow these few simple rules, and you too will be counted among the ranks of successful mutual fund investors!

Aggressive Growth Funds

AIM Constellation
800-347-4246 — 5.5% Front-End Load

This fund seeks capital appreciation by investing primarily in midsized companies. The fund has performed well during both bull and bear markets and, despite its front-end load, has served its investors well during the last decade.

Berger 100
800-333-1001 — 1% 12b-1 Fee

This fund invests in stocks of established companies with above-average earnings growth and return on equity. It is a highly volatile fund, as is the case with most earnings momentum investment strategies.

Columbia Special
800-547-1707 — No Load

Long-time portfolio manager Alan Folkman has produced better-than-average long-term returns by implementing a skillful sector rotation strategy. It is a highly volatile fund that performs best in bull markets.

Dreyfus Capital Growth
800-782-6620 — 3% Front-End Load

Formerly the Dreyfus Leverage Fund, this fund has been managed by Howard Stein since 1968. The fund may use leverage, sell short and invest up to 30 percent of its assets in foreign stocks.

Evergreen Limited Market
800-235-0064 — No Load

One of the true small-cap funds available to individual investors, it invests in little-known, small or special-situation companies for which limited trading markets exist. The fund has closed its doors to new investors from time to time.

Fidelity Growth Company
800-554-8888 3% Front-End Load

This fund, which began operations in 1983, seeks capital appreciation by investing in both large and small companies that management believes possess above-average growth characteristics.

Fidelity OTC Portfolio
800-554-8888 3% Front-End Load

This fund invests primarily in securities listed on Nasdaq, although it may invest up to 35 percent of its assets in exchange-listed securities. The fund has performed exceptionally well in bull stock markets.

Fidelity Trend
800-554-8888 No Load

This fund, established in 1959, seeks growth of capital by early identification of new growth trends. Management believes that the two keys to long-term success are diversification (investing in at least 50 companies in ten or more industries) and a fully invested position.

Founders Discovery
800-525-2440 0.25% 12b-1 Fee

The fund seeks capital appreciation by investing in small, rapidly growing U.S. companies. Its rapid earnings growth investment strategy has led to a concentration of assets in emerging growth industries such as computer software, technology and leisure time.

Growth Fund of America
800-421-9900 5.75% Front-End Load

This is one of the largest equity funds in the American Funds family. Its management team has shown a consistent ability to preserve capital in tough times and to prosper during rising markets.

Heartland Value
800-432-7856 No Load

Although a value investor, portfolio manager Bill Nasgovitz limits the fund's investments to companies with market capitalizations of less than $500 million. A good performer, the fund recently dropped its back-end sales charge and opted for no-load status.

Kaufmann Fund
800-237-0132 1% 12b-1 Fee

The fund's managers invest in small companies that are in substantial turnaround or in companies capable of growing by 30 percent or more each year. It possesses a higher-than-average expense ratio, but has produced enviable returns since current management assumed the reins in 1986.

Scudder Development
800-225-2470 No Load

With a beta of 1.50, this is one of the most volatile equity funds in the business. Its portfolio is tilted toward small-cap and medium-cap companies. As you would expect, it is capable of producing stellar returns during robust bull markets, but tends to suffer during market declines.

T. Rowe Price New Horizons
800-638-5660 No Load

This fund, which began operations in 1960, was the first fund to confine its investments to the small-cap sector of the market. With more than $1 billion in assets, fund management has been forced to allocate a large percentage of the fund's assets to mid-cap stocks in recent years.

T. Rowe Price OTC Securities
800-638-5660 No Load

Formerly owned by USF&G, Price became the fund's adviser in 1992. Since then, the fund has demonstrated better-than-average performance by concentrating its assets in small-cap and mid-cap growth stocks.

Twentieth Century Growth
800-345-2021 No Load

The fund is guided by a management team that sifts through the stocks of companies that pass a sophisticated computer screening process that emphasizes earnings momentum. It is a highly volatile fund that maintains a full investment posture at all times.

Twentieth Century Select
800-345-2021 No Load

The fund has one of the best 15-year performance records in the business. Its management team seeks seasoned, dividend-paying growth stocks whose sales and earnings are in an uptrend. It stays fully invested during both bull and bear stock markets.

Twentieth Century Ultra
800-345-2021 No Load

This fund, the most volatile domestic equity fund in the industry, is not for the feint of heart. Its share price soars in a bull market and tends to plummet in a bear market. It invests the bulk of its assets in small-cap to medium-cap earnings momentum stocks.

Value Line Fund
800-223-0818 No Load

The fund seeks long-term growth by basing stock selections on the Value Line Ranking System. This system ranks stocks on the basis of projected earnings, share price momentum and historical price levels. The portfolio tends to consist of mid-sized stocks with strong earnings growth.

Vanguard Explorer
800-635-1511 No Load

The fund's management stresses investment in smaller firms in the technology sector. It merged with Explorer II in 1990 and is now guided by dual portfolio managers. The fund possesses a low annual expense ratio and has maintained a modest portfolio turnover ratio in recent years.

Growth Funds

AIM Weingarten
800-347-4246 5.5% Front-End Load

This fund's portfolio is traditionally divided between established, stable growth stocks and stocks that show exceptional earnings growth. Its combination of steady growers and high-momentum cyclical stocks has produced excellent results in recent years.

AMCAP Fund
800-421-9900 — 5.75% Front-End Load

This fund epitomizes the all-weather performance that has become the signature of its adviser, Capital Research & Management. Rather than seek spectacular single-year gains, management attempts to produce acceptable results in both up and down markets.

Babson Value
800-422-2766 — No Load

Portfolio manager Nick Whitridge has guided this fund's fortunes since its inception in 1984. A patient investor, he seeks stocks with low price-earnings ratios, price-to-book values and price-to-sales ratios. He usually focuses on the blue chip sector of the market.

Brandywine Fund
800-338-1579 — No Load

This fund likes to own highly profitable niche companies with explosive growth potential. It normally draws investments from both the midcap and large-cap sectors of the market. It is a good performer; however, its $25,000 minimum initial investment limits the fund to investors with deep pockets.

Clipper Fund
800-776-5033 — No Load

An avowed value investor and asset allocator, portfolio manager James Gipson buys a stock only if he believes it is significantly underpriced relative to its underlying earnings power or asset value. His best results have come on big bets on companies in out-of-favor industries.

Columbia Growth
800-547-1707 — No Load

Espousing a rapid trading strategy, this fund's management team has obtained success where few do. Generally, moderate results are interspersed with an occasional banner year. Thus, you must be patient when investing in this fund.

Dreyfus Third Century
800-782-6620 No Load

Designed for socially conscious investors, this fund invests in common stocks of companies it believes contribute to the quality of life, and it has delivered solid returns in the process.

Evergreen Fund
800-235-0064 No Load

This fund, originally created to invest exclusively in small-cap stocks, has broadened its portfolio to include mid-cap, large-cap and blue chip stocks. Management prefers stocks with demonstrated solid earnings growth or those that possess hidden assets.

Fidelity Blue Chip Growth
800-544-8888 3% Front-End Load

This fund's affinity for rapid growth and above-average earnings momentum produces a portfolio packed with expensive, high- expectation stocks. Expect to be amply rewarded over the long run, but also expect a bumpy ride in the process.

Fidelity Contrafund
800-544-8888 3% Front-End Load

This fund owes its recent success to its moderate value orientation and its taste for healthy niche companies and turnarounds with unrecognized but solid earnings prospects.

Fidelity Fund
800-544-8888 No Load

This fund seeks capital appreciation with reasonable current income by investing in growth-oriented common stocks. It selects stocks solely on their own merits rather than by first drawing economic conclusions and making industry sector commitments.

Fidelity Magellan
800-544-8888 3% Front-End Load

With more than $30 billion in assets, this is the largest equity fund in the world. It attained its early success with the help of legendary portfolio manager Peter Lynch. Despite its gigantic size, the fund has consistently produced market-topping returns.

Founders Growth
800-525-2440 0.25% 12b-1 Fee

This fund's portfolio tends to be packed with established, quality companies boasting demonstrated records of above-average earnings growth. As a result, it emphasizes stocks in the health care, telecommunications, business services, financial and technology sectors of the market.

Janus Fund
800-525-3713 No Load

Portfolio manager James Craig has built an enviable reputation by making money during bull markets and preserving capital during bear markets. Historically, the fund has benefited from extremely well-timed retreats to cash.

Mutual Shares
800-448-3863 No Load

A value-oriented fund that stresses a combination of capital appreciation and current income, this fund is run by investment superstar Michael Price. At times, the fund has profited handsomely from Price's ability to spot value in bankruptcy or takeover situations.

Neuberger & Berman Guardian
800-877-9700 No Load

This fund's dual emphasis on growth and value usually enables it to produce highly competitive results in most markets. Its contrarian style suits patient investors who can wait for out-of-favor investments to return to vogue.

Neuberger & Berman Partners
800-877-9700 No Load

Giving top priority to capital preservation, this fund stresses relatively inexpensive growth stocks. Most of its investments show strong underlying fundamentals, but sell at depressed valuations because of negative market sentiment or temporary difficulties.

Nicholas Fund
414-272-6133 No Load

Most of this fund's quality companies show above-average earnings growth, high returns on equity, low leverage and strong franchises, but sell at low valuations. Portfolio manager Albert O. Nicholas has a knack for buying right and the patience to allow his investment selections to exhibit their true growth potential.

Oakmark Fund
800-476-9625 No Load

Established in 1991, this fund demonstrated performance during its first two years in business that was nothing short of spectacular. At the top of portfolio manager Robert Sanborn's selection criteria is a preference for companies whose stocks sell well below their book values.

Pennsylvania Mutual
800-221-4268 1% Redemption Fee

Although this fund is packed with small-cap stocks, portfolio manager Charles Royce is an avowed value player. His favorite stocks are those that sell at large discounts to their book values. Although selected for their growth potential, many of these stocks also pay generous cash dividends.

SAFECO Equity
800-624-5711 No Load

This fund seeks growth of capital by investing in mid-cap stocks that show above-average growth in earnings, but sell at modest valuations. The fund normally remains almost fully invested in both up and down markets.

SteinRoe Special
800-338-2550 No Load

This fund seeks maximum capital appreciation by investing in a mix of companies of various sizes and types. Typically, its portfolio features stocks with moderate to low price-earnings ratios.

Strong Common Stock
800-368-3863 No Load

Organized in 1989, this fund has benefited from its orientation to small-cap and mid-cap stocks. The fund has shown the same rapid trading techniques that market most of the other funds in the Strong family.

T. Rowe Price Growth Stock
800-638-5660 No Load

Most of this fund's investments show average growth in earnings and high profitability ratios. To keep risk moderate, its portfolio manager refuses to pay a high price-earnings multiple to acquire a stock. Thus, the fund tends to overweight out-of-favor growth industries.

Yacktman Fund
800-525-8258 0.15% 12b-1 Fee

Portfolio manager Donald Yacktman struck out on his own in 1992 after guiding the Selected American Shares Fund to a list-topping ten-year performance record. His investment style generally stresses the purchase of large-cap, blue chip growth stocks when they are out of favor with investors.

Growth and Income Funds

AARP Growth & Income
800-322-2282 No Load

This fund seeks current income and capital and income growth by investing in a mix of high-yielding common stocks and convertible securities. When selecting individual stocks, fund management requires a dividend yield of at least 20 percent more than that of the S&P 500 Index.

American Balanced
800-421-9900 5.75% Front-End Load

By investing in both stocks and bonds, this billion-dollar fund strives to meet three objectives: conservation of capital, current income and long-term growth of income and capital. Over the years, management has maintained a low portfolio turnover ratio, thus reducing trading costs and boosting current yield.

Dodge & Cox Balanced
415-434-0311 No Load

This fund seeks current income, capital appreciation and long-term growth of both capital and income by investing in stocks and bonds in a 60 percent/40 percent asset mix. It selects stocks for both their growth potential and their current dividend yield.

Evergreen Total Return
800-235-0064 No Load

Initiated in 1978, this conservative fund seeks a balance between current income and capital appreciation. Management allocates from 20 percent to 30 percent of the fund's assets to fixed-income securities and the balance to high-yielding common stocks.

Fidelity Balanced
800-544-8888 No Load

The investment objectives of this fund are preservation of capital and current income. The fund purchases high-yielding securities that include bonds, stocks and convertible securities. Management maintains at least 25 percent of the fund's assets in bonds rated BBB or better. Rarely have common stocks made up more than 50 percent of the fund's portfolio.

Fidelity Equity Income
800-544-8888 2% Front-End Load

This fund seeks reasonable yield by investing primarily in income-producing common stocks whose yields exceed the average yield of the stocks composing the S&P 500 Index and that also provide some capital appreciation potential.

Fidelity Puritan
800-544-8888 No Load

This balanced fund ideally suits conservative investors who seek current income and some capital appreciation. The portfolio tends to be divided 60/40 between stocks and bonds. Because of its relatively large allocation to bonds, the fund's share price tends to be somewhat sensitive to interest rate changes.

INVESCO Industrial Income
800-525-8085 No Load

Although this fund's objective is to provide current income and capital appreciation, capital appreciation has dominated in recent years. In addition to investing in high-yielding common stocks, the fund, at times, has assumed a hefty investment position in large-cap growth stocks.

Lindner Dividend
314-727-5305 No Load

This fund stresses a high level of current income. Thus, the portfolio generally contains only a few common stocks, with the bulk of its investments in convertible bonds, high-yield bonds, preferred stocks and some private placements.

Lindner Fund
314-727-5305 No Load

This fund, managed by Robert Lange since 1977, has consistently maintained a highly conservative bent. During the falling interest rates of the 1980s, this fund returned an average of more than 20 percent annually not only by achieving exceptional returns in up markets but by avoiding significant losses during down markets.

Oppenheimer Equity Income
800-525-7048 5.75% Front-End-Load

This vehicle, which stresses investment in high-yielding common stocks, has a beta of about one-half that of the stock market, an above-average current yield and a low expense ratio. It has been a steady performer during both good and bad stock markets.

Phoenix Balanced Fund
800-243-4361 4.75% Front-End Load

Like most growth and income funds, this fund seeks current income, long-term capital growth and conservation of capital. Stocks have traditionally accounted for about 60 percent of this fund's assets. Management has not hesitated to shift a substantial portion of fund assets to cash during down markets, thus offering a degree of protection not found in other balanced funds.

SAFECO Income
800-624-5711 No Load

This fund seeks to provide a combination of current income and capital growth by investing in common stocks with above-average dividend yields and in bonds. The equity portion of the portfolio tends to possess a value bent; thus, its performance usually suffers in growth stock-led bull markets.

Scudder Growth & Income
800-225-2470 No Load

Designed as a conservative fund, it seeks to provide current income and capital growth through investments in blue chip, dividend-paying common stocks and in bonds. In recent years, common stocks have tended to dominate the fund's investments.

SteinRoe Total Return
800-338-2550 No Load

This fund seeks to provide both capital appreciation and income. However, the income objective tends to dominate. Traditionally, the fund's portfolio has consisted of high-grade bonds. It is SteinRoe's oldest fund, with operations initiated in 1949.

Stratton Monthly Dividend Shares
800-441-6580 No Load

One of the few growth and income funds to distribute income monthly, this fund seeks a combination of current income and capital appreciation by investing primarily in high-yielding utility stocks and some convertible bonds. As a result, share price tends to be highly sensitive to interest rate changes.

Strong Investment
800-368-3863 No Load

The most conservative of the Strong family of equity funds, this fund invests in a diversified portfolio of common stocks, convertible bonds, preferred stocks and bonds. The allocation of assets to common stocks and convertible bonds may not exceed 65 percent of the fund's assets.

T. Rowe Price Equity Income
800-638-5660 No Load

Although similar to most other growth and income funds in its objectives (current income and capital appreciation), this fund leans toward the conservative in stressing a high dividend yield over capital growth. It invests primarily in the stocks of established companies that have favorable prospects for increasing their cash dividends.

T. Rowe Price Growth & Income
800-638-5660 No Load

This fund seeks current income and capital growth by investing in dividend-paying common stocks, preferred stocks and convertible bonds. Stocks are selected for both their current dividend yields and their relative valuations.

Twentieth Century Balanced
800-345-2021 No Load

A far cry from the typical balanced vehicle, this fund has all the earmarks of the potent, earnings momentum style that characterizes other Twentieth Century funds. Rapid, high-growth stocks tend to dominate the portfolio, with the balance held in various types of fixed-income securities.

United Income
913-236-2000 5.75% Front-End Load

This growth-and-income-seeking fund tends to allocate a significant portion of its assets to bonds and interest-bearing liquid assets. Although highly conservative, the fund has a share price that tends to be highly sensitive to changes in interest rates.

Value Line Income
800-223-0818 No Load

To achieve its primary objective—that is, a high level of current income—this fund invests in a mixture of stocks and bonds. When investing in common stocks, the fund relies heavily on the Value Line Ranking System.

Vanguard Equity Income
800-635-1511 No Load

This pure no-load fund seeks a high level of income by investing in a broad array of dividend-paying securities. Its goal is to produce a dividend yield that is at least 1.5 times that of the S&P 500 Index. A low portfolio turnover ratio and a very low expense ratio have enabled the fund to produce a current yield greater than those of its competitors.

Vanguard Star
800-635-1511 No Load

This unique fund invests in the shares of some of the best mutual funds in the Vanguard family. Investors pay no management fee or fund expenses. Instead, they assume a pro rata share of the expenses of the funds in its portfolio. It is a highly diversified, low-cost fund suitable for conservative investors.

Vanguard Wellington
800-635-1511 No Load

This established fund has provided investors with reasonable current income and preservation of principle for many years. Its conservative investments include high-yielding common stocks and investment-grade bonds.

International Equity Funds

Fidelity Europe
800-544-8888 3% Front-End Load

By investing in the securities of companies whose principal business activities take place in Western Europe, the fund strives to obtain growth of capital. Like most regional funds, it has a share price that is more volatile than the share price of the well-diversified international fund.

Fidelity Overseas
800-544-8888 3% Front-End Load

This fund has performed very well since its inception in 1984. During the latter part of the 1980s, the fund benefited from a large investment position in Japanese common stocks. Like most well-diversified international funds, its performance suffered during the early 1990s as most major world stock markets gave ground.

Fidelity Pacific Basin
800-544-8888 3% Front-End Load

This fund invests in the securities of companies that operate in Australia, China, Hong Kong, India, Japan, Korea, Malaysia, New Zealand, the Philippines, Singapore, Taiwan and Thailand. Because most of these countries can be described as emerging markets, the fund possesses a high degree of risk.

G.T. Worldwide Growth
800-824-1580 4.75% Front-End Load

Although the portfolio tends to contain heavy allocations to Japanese and U.S. securities, the fund makes plenty of room for emerging growth, secondary markets such as Singapore and Mexico, as well as European markets such as Germany and France. It is the most broadly defined fund in the G.T. Global family.

INVESCO Strategic European
800-525-8085 No Load

The assets of this fund are invested primarily in securities of companies domiciled in Europe. The fund is biased toward large- cap, better established issues, which have fared better than the typical international stock during the last decade.

Ivy International
800-777-6472 5.75% Front-End Load

This fund is proof that slow and steady wins the race. Patient management seeks stocks that sell at discounts to their underlying fundamentals and avoids chasing hot markets and sectors. Its long-term approach and low portfolio turnover have aided performance in recent years.

Montgomery Emerging Markets

800-572-3863 No Load

Aggressively seeking capital appreciation, this fund invests mainly in equity securities of companies based in emerging economies around the world. Management shapes the portfolio by allocating assets to emerging markets based on their relative sizes. After setting country allocations, management selects individual stocks for their fundamental values.

Oakmark International

800-476-9625 No Load

Since its inception in 1992, this fund has been one of the hottest funds in the international equities category. Although it may invest anywhere in the world, more than half of its assets have been fairly evenly spread across European countries.

Oppenheimer Global

800-525-7048 5.75% Front-End Load

This fund seeks primarily capital appreciation by investing in worldwide growth companies. Returns have been consistently above average in recent years. Lately, its new portfolio manager has added investments in emerging markets. The fund may at times allocate a significant portion of assets to U.S. stocks.

Scudder International

800-225-2470 No Load

This fund is one of the oldest in the international equity category. It is a large and well-diversified fund that has benefited in recent years from a steady decline in the value of the dollar. It is one of the least volatile funds in the international equities category.

Templeton Developing Markets

800-354-9191 5.75% Front-End Load

Recently acquired by Franklin Securities, the fund has retained the Templeton management team. With a concentration of assets in emerging markets in Latin America and the Pacific Rim, this fund contains more risk than the typical international equities fund. However, with growth potential twice that of developed countries, these markets should produce stellar returns if you have the patience to hold your investment in this fund for several years.

Templeton World
800-345-9191 5.75% Front-End Load

The largest equity fund in the Templeton group (now owned by Franklin Securities), the fund can invest in both equity and debt securities of any company in the world. In the past, the fund has invested a significant portion of its assets in U.S. stocks.

T. Rowe Price International Stock
800-638-5660 No Load

This old and established fund avoids U.S. stocks and maintains a presence in at least 20 countries at any given time. Like most international funds, it stresses macroeconomic themes and above- average growth markets. Recently, the fund has maintained a modest allocation to stocks traded in emerging markets.

Twentieth Century International
800-345-2021 No Load

This relatively new fund, established in 1991, seeks the stocks of rapidly growing companies no matter where in the world they may be domiciled. Geographic placement is a secondary consideration in the fund's stock selection process. As one might expect from a high-growth-potential equity portfolio, the fund's shares possess relatively high price volatility.

Vanguard International Growth
800-635-1511 No Load

This fund diversifies its assets among about 30 foreign markets. The fund seeks companies with above-average earnings prospects that have unrecognized value in their respective markets. Like most funds in the Vanguard family, it possesses a low annual expense ratio and a no-load format.

Precious Metals Funds

Benham Gold Equities Index
800-472-3389 No Load

This fund strives to duplicate the returns of an index of North American gold stocks by investing at least 85 percent of its assets in companies included in the index. The fund may invest up to 10 percent of its assets in gold, certificates of ownership or gold futures.

Fidelity Select Precious Metals
800-544-8888 3% Front-End Load

This fund invests about half of its assets in South American and Australian gold stocks, with the balance invested in North American gold producers. The fund stresses top-quality, major gold producers and avoids secondary gold stocks and exploration plays.

Lexington Goldfund
800-526-0056 0.20% 12b-1 Fee

Among the more tame of precious metals portfolios, this fund attempts to temper the volatility associated with gold investing by adjusting its asset mix in response to market conditions. Besides raising its cash and bullion exposure when gold prices are unfavorable, it avoids the stocks of smaller, highly leveraged producers.

Lexington Strategic Investments
800-526-0056 5.75% Front-End Load

Lexington assumed the role of investment adviser in March 1992. Prior to that, the fund had posted one of the worst performance records in its category. The fund is packed with small South African mining companies and, not surprisingly, is the most volatile fund in its category. However, its much better performance has accompanied the recent change in management.

United Services Gold Shares
800-873-8637 No Load

Investing exclusively in South African gold stocks, this fund is among the most volatile in its category. Although these stocks possess hefty dividend yields, they are prone to sharp price swings in response to both gold price movements and changes in South Africa's political climate.

Sector Funds

Century Shares Trust

800-321-1928 No Load

This fund, which began operations in 1928, seeks capital appreciation by investing primarily in insurance stocks. Like insurance stocks generally, the fund provides a better-than-average dividend yield and is highly sensitive to changes in interest rates.

Fidelity Select Electric Utilities

800-544-8888 3% Front-End Load

As the name suggests, this fund concentrates its portfolio in electric utility stocks while attempting to provide both current income and growth of capital. In addition, it holds investments in companies with operations related to electric utilities, such as construction, pollution control and waste disposal.

Fidelity Select Health Care

800-544-8888 3% Front-End Load

This highly volatile fund seeks growth of capital by concentrating its portfolio in health-care-related stocks such as pharmaceuticals, medical equipment and supplies, and medical facilities management.

Fidelity Select Technology

800-544-8888 3% Front-End Load

One of the original select portfolios, this fund seeks capital appreciation by investing in a relatively concentrated portfolio of technology stocks, including aerospace, cellular communications, computer services and software, electronics and medical equipment and supplies.

Franklin Utilities

800-342-5236 4% Front-End Load

One of the highest yielding equity funds in the industry, this fund has traditionally overweighted electric utility stocks in the pursuit of its twin objectives of current income and capital growth. A low annual expense ratio and an extremely low portfolio turnover ratio mitigate the fund's 4 percent front-end sales charge.

INVESCO Strategic Health Sciences
800-525-8085 No Load

This fund's investments span a wide variety of firms, ranging from staid pharmaceutical companies to exotic biotechnology concerns. Like most capital-appreciation-oriented industry sector funds, share price can be extremely volatile.

T. Rowe Price Science & Technology
800-638-5660 No Load

This fund seeks growth of capital through investments in companies expected to benefit from the development, advancement and utilization of science and technology. It has substantial exposure to small-cap companies experiencing very rapid earnings growth.

Vanguard Specialized Health Care
800-635-1511 No Load

This fund seeks capital appreciation by investing in the stocks of health care and health-care-related companies. The fund has maintained a large-cap bias and possesses the lowest volatility among health care industry sector funds.

Vanguard Specialized Technology
800-635-1511 No Load

Concentrating in the stocks of companies related to advances in technology, the fund invests with a view to the longer term. The bulk of its assets tend to be concentrated in software, data processing, computers, communications, electronics and aerospace stocks.

Vanguard Specialized Utilities
800-635-1511 No Load

A relatively new addition to the Vanguard Specialized Portfolios, this fund invests in both equity and debt securities of companies engaged in generating and distributing electricity, gas, telecommunications or water. A conservative growth and income fund, it selects assets for their fundamental value.

Appendix

Sources of Mutual Fund Information and Advice

One of the requirements for investment success is informed decisions. With more than 6,000 mutual funds to select from these days, it is pure folly to believe that you can assemble a portfolio of funds that will allow you to accomplish your financial objectives without adequate investigation and analysis. Of course, some investors merely follow their stockbrokers' advice and buy whatever funds the brokers happen to be selling that month. Other investors become enamored with a fund because it or its manager has been written up in the financial press. Although you might end up with some pretty good funds if you make your selections this way, chances are you will acquire a portfolio that is ill-suited to your investment objectives and financial needs.

Rather than assemble a portfolio haphazardly, you might apply a disciplined procedure. First, outline your investment needs and objectives. Second, determine the types of funds that you believe will serve these needs. Third, obtain data for several funds of each type. Fourth, rate the funds by type, and select the top-rated funds for your portfolio. Finally, once you have assembled your portfolio, monitor individual fund performance and operating characteristics. Replace poorly performing funds and those whose operating characteristics no longer contribute to your investment objectives or your preferred investment style.

Note that each phase of the mutual fund selection and portfolio management process requires information about the funds available to you. So, before you select your first mutual fund, spend a little time and a few dollars obtaining the information you will need to make intelligent decisions. Believe me, the time, effort and money you spend learning about the funds that eventually wind up in your portfolio will pay off handsomely.

Mutual fund information comes from a variety of sources. Two companies, Morningstar and Value Line, publish extensive data for nearly 2,000 open-end funds. Every two weeks, subscribers receive updates for about 100 funds. Everything you would ever want to know about a fund (and much that you probably don't need to know) is presented in their basic packages. Be prepared to spend about $300 for an annual subscription to these services. Although the services are comprehensive, they may not be cost effective for many individual investors. You can obtain a much better deal by investing a few dollars in a mutual fund almanac or encyclopedia, which you can get at any reasonably sized bookstore. These publications describe the financial characteristics and track the historical performance of hundreds of funds. They are ideal sources of data for investors who wish to make their own investment decisions. The price of these publications ranges from $25 to $50. The reference works are updated annually, and new editions usually appear on bookstore shelves in March or April.

You also may want to consider subscribing to one or two mutual fund advisory newsletters. Generally, these newsletters contain model portfolios for various investment objectives, provide lists of recommended funds and present topical research on various categories of funds. Some mutual fund advisory newsletters provide investment hotlines that update their fund recommendations and financial market outlooks daily or weekly. A number of advisory newsletters also offer portfolio management services. Users of these services grant the investment adviser limited power of attorney to trade their accounts, which are usually established at discount brokerage firms. The minimum initial investment requirement for managed accounts ranges from approximately $50,000 to $100,000. The annual fees for such services range from 1 percent to 2 percent of the portfolio's value. Managed accounts ideally suite investors who either don't have the time to manage their own mutual fund portfolios or lack the confidence to make individual fund selections.

The following list of publications provides a sample of the types of information and advisory services available to mutual fund investors. Many newsletter publishers will send you a recent sample issue free of charge if you request one. Most public libraries subscribe to either *Morningstar* or *Value Line*. You can obtain annual almanacs and encyclopedias at your favorite bookstore.

Advisory Newsletters

Donoghue's Moneyletter
P.O. Box 6640
Holliston, MA 01746
Tel: 508-429-5930

Editor: Daniel Bates
Frequency: Twice monthly
Since: 1980

Fidelity Insight
Mutual Fund Investors Assn.
P.O. Box 9135
Wellesley, MA 02181
Tel: 800-444-6342

Editor: Eric Kobren
Frequency: Monthly
Since: 1987

Fidelity Monitor
P.O. Box 1294
Rocklin, CA 95677
Tel: 800-397-3094

Editor: Jack Bowers
Frequency: Monthly
Since: 1986

Fund Exchange
1200 Westlake Ave. N.
Suite 700
Seattle, WA 98109
Tel: 206-285-8877

Editor: Paul Merriman
Frequency: Monthly
Since: 1983

InvesTech Mutual Fund Advisor
2472 Birch Glen
Whitefish, MT 59937
Tel: 800-955-8500

Editor: James Stack
Frequency: 17 times annually
Since: 1985

Mutual Fund Forecaster
3471 N. Federal Highway
Fort Lauderdale, FL 33306
Tel: 800-442-9000

Editor: Norman Fosback
Frequency: Monthly
Since: 1985

Mutual Fund Investing
7811 Montrose Rd.
Potomac, MD 20854
Tel: 800-722-9000

Editor: Jay Shabacker
Frequency: Monthly
Since: 1985

The Mutual Fund Letter
680 N. Lake Shore Dr.
Tower Suite 2038
Chicago, IL 60611
Tel: 800-326-6941

Editor: Gerald W. Perritt
Frequency: Monthly
Since: 1984

No-Load Fund Investor
1 Bridge St.
Irving-on- Hudson, NY 10533
Tel: 914-693-7420

Editor: Sheldon Jacobs
Frequency: Monthly
Since: 1978

No-Load Fund X
235 Montgomery St.
San Francisco, CA 94104
Tel: 415-986-7979

Editor: Burt Berry
Frequency: Monthly
Since: 1976

Mutual Fund Data Subscription Services

Morningstar Mutual Funds
225 W. Wacker Dr.
Chicago, IL 60606
Tel: 800-876-500

Value Line Mutual Fund Survey
220 E. 42nd St.
New York, NY 10017
Tel: 800-284-7607

Mutual Fund Annuals

Handbook for No-Load Fund Investors
Sheldon Jacobs
No-Load Fund Investor

Individual Investors Guide to Low-Load Mutual Funds
American Association of Individual Investors

The Mutual Fund Encyclopedia
Gerald W. Perritt
Dearborn Financial Publishing

Glossary

account statement A document sent to shareholders of a fund that indicates the number of shares held, lists recent purchases and notes fund distributions. Statements are usually sent after a purchase is made and then annually thereafter.

adviser The organization (usually the fund's sponsor) employed by a fund to give professional advice regarding the fund's investments. The adviser receives an annual fee, ranging from 0.50 percent to 1 percent of the fund's assets. The adviser absorbs the cost of maintaining its offices, statistical services and other expenses related to its portfolio management activities.

annual and semiannual reports The documents sent to a fund's shareholders that discuss the fund's recent investment performance, provides its financial and operating statistics and lists the securities in the fund's portfolio.

ARM funds Bond funds that invest in adjustable-rate mortgages. These are mortgages whose interest rates are periodically reset to reflect current conditions in the mortgage market. Some funds invest in government-backed mortgages only, such as GNMAs. Others invest in private mortgages and financial derivatives, such as interest-only or principal-only STRIPS.

asked or offering price The price at which a mutual fund's shares are purchased. For no-load funds, the offering price is the fund's per-share net asset value. For front-end load funds, the offering price includes the dealer's mark-up or sales charge.

automatic reinvestment plan A shareholder-authorized share purchase plan that allows a fund to reinvest all income and capital gains distributions in additional fund shares instead of sending cash payments to the shareholder. Although reinvested in additional fund shares, distributions create tax liabilities for tax-paying shareholders.

back-end load Sales charge levied on the amount actually invested in a fund upon withdrawal of that investment. Some back-end loads are referred to as contingent deferred sales charges because the amount of the charge is reduced each year that the initial investment remains in the fund, usually being eliminated after a five-year holding period.

balanced fund A fund whose investment objective is both current income and growth of capital. In seeking to meet this objective, such a fund invests in a combination of bonds and common stocks.

beta A statistical measure of a mutual fund's return volatility (risk) relative to that of the stock market as a whole, which is usually proxied by the Standard & Poor's 500 Index. A fund with a beta of 1.20 is 20 percent more volatile than the market, while a fund with a beta of 0.80 would be 20 percent less volatile than the stock market.

bid price The price at which the shares of a mutual fund are redeemed (bought back) by the fund. The bid or redemption price usually equals the fund's per-share net asset value. However, this amount can be reduced by back-end sales charges.

blue chip A phrase given to large-capitalization stocks of well-respected old-line companies. The name is derived from the highest denomination chip used in games of poker.

blue-sky laws The securities laws to which mutual funds must conform in each of the states in which they sell shares to the public. These state laws govern both the operations of a fund and the distribution and advertising of fund shares sold within a state.

capital gains distribution A distribution of the net realized gains on securities held by a fund. Realized losses are deducted from realized gains each year, and the net difference, if any, is distributed to shareholders, usually in late December. The fund's share price declines by the amount of the distribution on the ex-distribution date.

classes of shares Classes of the shares of a single portfolio distinguished by the type of sales charge levied by the fund. For example, class A shares carry a front-end load, class B shares possess a contingent deferred sales charge, class C shares levy an annual 12b-1 charge and so on.

closed-end fund An entity actually classified as an investment company rather than a fund by U.S. securities laws that limits the number of shares issued. Instead of buying shares directly from the fund, investors must obtain closed-end shares from other investors. Most are listed on the New York Stock Exchange or the American Stock Exchange. Price is determined by supply and demand and may be above (a premium) or below (a discount) that of the fund's per-share net asset value.

contingent deferred sales charge *See* back-end load.

contractual plan A plan offered by most funds sold with a sales charge whereby an individual agrees to invest a fixed amount on a regular basis for a specified number of years. Generally, a large portion of the total sales charges is deducted from the amounts invested early in the program.

custodian The organization, usually a bank, that has custody of securities and other fund assets. These days, the ownership of most securities is kept in book entry form.

distributions The payment of income and capital gains to shareholders. It is also a term used to describe how a fund is marketed.

diversification The policy of all mutual funds to spread investments among a number of assets in order to reduce portfolio risk. Diversification works best when the returns of the securities held are less than perfectly correlated with one another. Thus, the losses incurred by securities falling in price are offset by gains of those rising in price. This is the largest benefit of mutual fund investing.

diversified investment company A mutual fund that invests its assets so that at least 75 percent of its total assets are invested in securities, with not more than 5 percent of its assets invested in the securities of any one issuer, and not holding more than 10 percent of the voting securities of any one corporation.

dollar cost averaging The practice of investing equal dollar amounts at regular intervals. This procedure reduces the average price of each share purchased because more shares are purchased when prices fall and less are purchased when prices rise. It's one sure way to increase fund investments when prices fall.

exchange privilege An option provided by mutual fund families that allows investors to transfer their investments from one of the family's funds to another, usually by telephone. Although shares in one fund are exchanged for shares in another, the exchange is treated by the IRS as a sale and subsequent purchase; thus, a tax liability could result on realized gains.

expense ratio The ratio of a mutual fund's total annual expenses (including management fees) to total assets. This percentage indicates how much fund operating costs reduce annual investment returns. Generally, the annual expense ratios of bond funds average about 0.80 percent. The average expense ratios of equity funds vary depending on the nature of a fund and fund size. (Larger funds tend to possess lower expense ratios.) The average expense ratio for diversified equity funds is about 1 percent and about 1.5 percent for specialized equity funds and international equity funds.

family of funds A group of mutual funds, usually with different investment objectives and investment strategies, managed and distributed by the same company. Most fund families offer telephone exchange privileges to shareholders.

front-end load A sales charge levied on the initial purchase of the shares of some funds. The charge is said to be "loaded" because the percentage sales fee is deducted from the amount of the purchase, with the net amount actually being invested in fund shares. For example, an 8 percent front-end load increases to 9.15 percent when based on the actual amount invested in fund shares after the deduction of sales charges.

index funds Passively managed funds that attempt to capture the returns of an index of either stock or bond prices. Index funds usually invest in securities in an attempt to replicate the construction of the underlying indexes. Because these funds are passively managed, they tend to have lower expenses and turnover ratios than actively managed funds.

individual retirement account (IRA) A savings plan that defers the taxes on income and capital gains earned on investments until they are withdrawn from the plan. Individuals not covered by any other retirement plan may make tax-deductible contributions (not exceeding $2,000 per year) to their IRAs. Withdrawals made before a participant reaches age 59½ are subject to a 10 percent early withdrawal penalty.

investment company A financial institution that exists solely for the purpose of investing in a portfolio of assets. Investment companies include unit investment trusts, mutual funds, closed-end funds and real estate investment trusts.

load The amount of a sales fee levied on either the purchase or sale of fund shares. *See* front-end load and back-end load.

low-load A somewhat nebulous term used to identify mutual funds with sales charges that are less than the maximum allowable by law. Usually, low-load refers to a fund with a front-end or back-end load of less than 4 percent.

management company The most plentiful member of the investment company family. They include closed-end funds, open-end (mutual) funds and real estate investment trusts. They are distinguished from unit investment trusts because their portfolios are usually actively managed.

management fee The amount paid to a fund's adviser for its services. These fees are accrued daily and paid monthly to the fund's adviser. Fees range from 0.50 percent to 1 percent for most funds.

money market fund A mutual fund that invests in securities with short-term maturities (90 days or less). Share price is fixed at $1 and interest is reinvested in additional shares daily. Some money market funds invest in government securities only, while others invest in securities issued by banks and large corporations. Most money market funds extend check-writing privileges to shareholders.

mutual fund A corporation chartered by a particular state that pools shareholder capital and invests in a portfolio of securities. It is "mutual" because the fund is actually owned by its shareholders, who pay a pro rata share of fund operating expenses and receive a pro rata share of income earned and capital gains realized.

net asset value (NAV) The value of a mutual fund share. It is derived by aggregating the value of a fund's total assets (securities, cash and accrued earnings), deducting liabilities and dividing by the number of shares outstanding. Per-share net asset value is the same as share price for no-load mutual funds.

no-load fund A mutual fund whose shares are sold without sales charges of any kind. Some no-load funds levy a 1 percent redemption charge for investments held less than six months.

open-end investment company A mutual fund that continually sells new shares to investors and redeems those that are tendered by shareholders. Unlike a closed-end fund, its capitalization is not fixed. Some funds restrict the sales of new shares to current shareholders only.

portfolio turnover ratio A measure of the trading activity of a mutual fund. It gives an indication of how frequently securities are bought and sold. It is computed by taking the lesser of purchases and sales of securities and dividing by the fund's average net assets. The reciprocal of the turnover ratio can be used to approximate the fund's average securities holding period. For example, a fund with an 80 percent turnover ratio holds its investments an average of 1.25 years. (1/0.80 = 1.25)

prospectus The legal document that describes a mutual fund's investment objectives, risks, investment limitations, policies, services and fees. It must be furnished to all fund investors.

redemption price The price at which a fund buys back its shares from selling shareholders. The redemption price may be reduced by back-end loads.

registered investment company An investment company registered with the Securities and Exchange Commission and governed by the Investment Company Act of 1940.

Securities and Exchange Commission (SEC) The primary U.S. federal government agency that regulates registration and distribution of mutual fund shares.

statement of additional information (SAI) Also called Part B of a fund's registration statement. It contains more detailed, supplementary information about a mutual fund. It is available at no charge upon request from a fund.

transfer agent The organization employed by a mutual fund to prepare and maintain records relating to the accounts of its shareholders. Although these services are usually provided by a fund's custodian bank, some funds serve as their own transfer agents.

12b-1 fee An annual mutual fund sales charge levied on investments in the fund. Named after the SEC rule that allowed funds to begin charging annual distribution fees, 12b-1 fees range from 0.10 percent to as much as 0.75 percent of a fund's assets.

unit investment trust An investment company that purchases a fixed portfolio of income-producing securities (i.e., the portfolio of securities is not traded) with a specific maturity date. Units are sold to investors by brokers.

unrealized appreciation or depreciation Increases or decreases in the prices of securities held by a fund.

variable annuity An investment contract sold to an investor by an insurance company. Capital is accumulated, usually by investment in a mutual fund, and is converted to an income stream payable to the annuity holder at a future date. It is variable because the eventual income payments vary with the value of the account. Annuities also include charges for insurance that guarantees the minimum payment of a lump sum in the event of an investor's death.

withdrawal plan A program in which shareholders receive payments from their mutual fund investments at regular intervals.

Index